D1462765

VOLUME 13

JEREMIAH and LAMENTATIONS

Linda B. Hinton

ABINGDON PRESS
Nashville

Jeremiah and Lamentations

Copyright © 1988 by Graded Press

This book is printed on recycled, acid-free paper.

Library of Congress Cataloging-in-Publication Data

Cokesbury basic Bible commentary.
    Basic Bible commentary / by Linda B. Hinton . . . [et.al.].
      p.   cm.
    Originally published: Cokesbury basic Bible commentary. Nashville: Graded Press, © 1988.
    ISBN 0-687-02620-2 (pbk. : v. 1 : alk. paper)
    1. Bible—Commentaries. I. Hinton, Linda B. II. Title.
    [BS491.2.C65   1994]
    220.7—dc20
                                           94-10965
                                                CIP

ISBN 0-687-02632-6 (v. 13, Jeremiah–Lamentations)
ISBN 0-687-02620-2 (v. 1, Genesis)
ISBN 0-687-02621-0 (v. 2, Exodus–Leviticus)
ISBN 0-687-02622-9 (v. 3, Numbers–Deuteronomy)
ISBN 0-687-02623-7 (v. 4, Joshua–Ruth)
ISBN 0-687-02624-5 (v. 5, 1–2 Samuel)
ISBN 0-687-02625-3 (v. 6, 1–2 Kings)
ISBN 0-687-02626-1 (v. 7, 1–2 Chronicles)
ISBN 0-687-02627-X (v. 8, Ezra–Esther)
ISBN 0-687-02628-8 (v. 9, Job)
ISBN 0-687-02629-6 (v. 10, Psalms)
ISBN 0-687-02630-X (v. 11, Proverbs–Song of Solomon)
ISBN 0-687-02631-8 (v. 12, Isaiah)
ISBN 0-687-02633-4 (v. 14, Ezekiel–Daniel)
ISBN 0-687-02634-2 (v. 15, Hosea–Jonah)
ISBN 0-687-02635-0 (v. 16, Micah–Malachi)
ISBN 0-687-02636-9 (v. 17, Matthew)
ISBN 0-687-02637-7 (v. 18, Mark)
ISBN 0-687-02638-5 (v. 19, Luke)
ISBN 0-687-02639-3 (v. 20, John)
ISBN 0-687-02640-7 (v. 21, Acts)
ISBN 0-687-02642-3 (v. 22, Romans)
ISBN 0-687-02643-1 (v. 23, 1–2 Corinthians)
ISBN 0-687-02644-X (v. 24, Galatians–Ephesians)
ISBN 0-687-02645-8 (v. 25, Philippians–2 Thessalonians)
ISBN 0-687-02646-6 (v. 26, 1 Timothy–Philemon)
ISBN 0-687-02647-4 (v. 27, Hebrews)
ISBN 0-687-02648-2 (v. 28, James–Jude)
ISBN 0-687-02649-0 (v. 29, Revelation)
ISBN 0-687-02650-4 (complete set of 29 vols.)

99 00 01 02 03—10 9 8 7 6 5 4 3 2

MANUFACTURED IN THE UNITED STATES OF AMERICA

Contents

Outline of Jeremiah and Lamentations

Jeremiah

I. Introduction and Call to Prophesy (1:1-10)
II. Vision Reports and Oracles Against the People of Israel (1:11–25:14)
    A. Reports and Oracles From the Time of King Josiah (1:11–6:30)
        1. Vision Reports (1:11-19)
        2. Oracles Against Unfaithful Israel (2:1-37)
        3. Oracles Calling Israel to Repent (3:1–4:4)
        4. Oracles About the Foe from the North (4:5-31)
        5. The Search for Truth and Justice in Israel Is Futile (5:1-31)
        6. The Foe From the North Approaches (6:1-30)
    B. Reports and Oracles From the Time of King Jehoiakim (7:1–20:18)
        1. Oracles Concerning the Temple (7:1–8:3)
        2. Oracles Against Israel and a Lament for Her Fate (8:4–9:1)
        3. Lamentations Over the People of Israel (9:2-26)
        4. Oracles Against Idols and a Plea for Mercy (10:1-25)
        5. Jeremiah and the Covenant (11:1-17)
        6. Jeremiah Laments His Fate (11:18–12:6)
        7. Lamentation for Judah (12:7-17)
        8. Pride and Sin Bring Punishment (13:1-27)
        9. Lamentation Over Judah (14:1–15:9)
       10. Jeremiah's Second Personal Lament (15:10-21)

Lamentations

Introduction to Jeremiah

The prophetic ministry of Jeremiah began in 627 B.C. during the reign of the Judean king Josiah (640–609 B.C.) when Jeremiah was only a youth. His ministry continued until around 580 B.C. and ended in Egypt. Jeremiah was one of the major prophets of ancient Israel. Much of his life and many of his words are recorded in the Old Testament book that bears his name. His personal story is interwoven with his prophecy and with the story of the people of Israel.

The years of Jeremiah's ministry were turbulent and tragic years for Israel. Jeremiah's prophecy must be seen against this background. He addressed specific circumstances in the life of Israel, and he delivered God's messages concerning these circumstances.

Historical Backgrounds

After the death of King Solomon, the kingdom of Israel was divided into Israel in the north and Judah in the south. (*Israel* sometimes means specifically the Northern Kingdom. Israel can also mean *the people of Israel*, which includes all the chosen people in the north and in the south.) The Northern Kingdom was conquered by Assyria in 722 B.C.

When Assyria's power declined, King Josiah of Judah extended his power into parts of the Northern Kingdom. Josiah also initiated a religious reform in Judah. This reform sought to rid Israelite faith and practice of the pagan rituals that had been introduced in years past.

Worship was purified and centralized into the Temple in Jerusalem. Shrines and sanctuaries in outlying areas were closed.

Josiah's reign ended when he was killed in battle at Megiddo in 609 B.C. His son, Jehoahaz, took his place but was deposed by the Egyptians, who put Jehoahaz's brother, Jehoiakim (Eliakim), on the throne. The religious reforms of Josiah were soon forgotten.

During this time, Babylonia was becoming a world power. By 603 B.C., Jehoiakim and Judah were under Babylonian control. Jehoiakim tried to break away from Babylon in 601 B.C. to establish Judah as an independent state once again.

In December 598 B.C., the Babylonian army besieged Jerusalem. Jehoiakim was killed and his son, Jehoiachin, soon surrendered the city. Hundreds of Israelites were deported to Babylon, including the king, his court, priests, artisans, and other leading citizens. Zedekiah, the uncle of Jehoiachin, was made king under Babylonian control.

Judah rebelled in 588 B.C. and, once again, Babylonian forces attacked Jerusalem. The city fell in 587 B.C. after an eighteen-month siege. More Israelites were deported and the city was destroyed.

King Nebuchadrezzar of Babylon appointed Gedaliah, a member of a prominent Judean family, as provincial governor. Gedaliah was assassinated in 582 B.C. by a zealous member of the Judean royal family. Fearing reprisals from the Babylonians for Gedaliah's death, some Israelites fled to Egypt. Jeremiah was forced to go with them. More captives were taken from Judah to Babylon, and the hardship of those left in Judah increased.

In 539 B.C., Persia defeated Babylonia. Cyrus, the Persian king, gave the exiled Israelites permission to return to Judah. Jeremiah did not live to see this return. His prophecy, however, helped pave the way for Israel's

JEREMIAH AND LAMENTATIONS

survival as a community of faith by dealing with Israel's disaster within the context of faith.

Important Dates for the Book of Jeremiah

722 B.C. — Northern Kingdom absorbed by Assyria
687–642 B.C. — Manasseh king of Judah
642–640 B.C. — Amon king of Judah
640–609 B.C. — Josiah king of Judah
627 B.C.— Jeremiah called to prophesy
612 B.C. — Babylonians conquer the Assyrian capital
609 B.C. — Jehoahaz king of Judah, deposed by Egypt
609–598 B.C. — Jehoiakim king of Judah
605 B.C. — Babylonians defeat Egyptians and Assyrians at Carchemish; extend influence over Judah
601 B.C. — Jehoiakim rebels against Babylon
598–597 B.C. — Babylonian siege of Jerusalem; Jehoiakim killed
598–597 B.C. — Jehoiachin king of Judah; Jerusalem surrenders; many Israelites deported to Babylon.
597–587 B.C. — Jedekiah king of Judah
588–587 B.C. — Judah rebels; Babylonian siege of Jerusalem; Jerusalem destroyed; more Israelites deported
587–582 B.C. — Gedaliah appointed governor of Judah
582 B.C. — Gedaliah assassinated, Jeremiah forced into exile in Egypt.

(Note concerning dates: Remember that some dates are known precisely and others are only approximate. Historical sources will frequently vary as much as a year or two in giving some dates. Most ancient documents have been lost or destroyed, so there are not many sources of information other than the Bible for this time in history. This situation is complicated by the fact that ancient systems of dating do not correspond to our present calendar. Also, not all ancient dating systems are alike. Keep these factors in mind as you study the history of Israel, especially when you find references which give differing dates for the same event.)

Jeremiah the Man

Jeremiah was born into a priestly family sometime around 645 B.C. His father, Hilkiah, was a descendant of the priest Abiathar who had been banished to his ancestral home in Anathoth by King Solomon. (See 1 Kings 2:26-27.)

In a priestly family, Jeremiah was taught Israel's ancient traditions and the words of Israel's prophets. We do not know whether he received formal training as a priest.

At his call to prophesy, Jeremiah calls himself a boy (NRSV; NIV = *child*). This may or may not mean that he was a very young man. It may merely indicate that he felt himself too immature for the task God assigned to him. He must have been a relatively young man at the time, though, because his recorded ministry spanned forty-seven years.

At first Jeremiah tried to escape the claim of God's call. He must have understood the burden and personal cost of fulfilling such a call. In later years, he expressed contempt for those people who embraced the office of prophet without appreciating the gravity of it. At times, Jeremiah hated his calling and longed to quit his duties as God's spokesman. He even confronted God with the terrible burdens he bore for God's sake. But he could not push God's word away.

To fulfill his duties, Jeremiah had to forgo a wife and children of his own. He had to suffer hatred, misunderstanding, and physical abuse. At times his life was threatened. His message of judgment against Israel often disagreed with popular belief and official theology.

Though Jeremiah is often remembered as a sorrowful and gloomy man, he also offered words of hope and comfort to Israel. He was commissioned by God not only put *pluck up* and *to tear down* but also *to build and to plant*.

Jeremiah the Book

The book of Jeremiah is a collection of different kinds of material. It contains prophetic oracles from Jeremiah's public preaching, prayers, stories about Jeremiah, vision reports, sermons, laments, and historical narratives. Some of the book is prose and some is poetry.

The collection was started during Jeremiah's ministry and was finished sometime after 560 B.C. Baruch, Jeremiah's friend and scribe, wrote much of the material in the collection. Jeremiah may have had other disciples or scribes who helped record his words and life.

The book has the following sections:
   (1) Oracles Against Judah and Jerusalem, 1:1–25:14
   (2) Biographical Narratives, chapters 26–29; 34–45
   (3) Oracles of Consolation and Hope, chapters 30–31
   (4) Oracles Against Foreign Nations, 25:15-38; chapters 45–51
   (5) Historical Appendix, chapter 52

A Word of Caution

Keep in mind that the book of Jeremiah is the record of material which, for the most part, was originally spoken instead of written. These oracles, sermons, and laments were delivered over a period of approximately forty-seven years. Their present written order and relationships are not always in chronological order. Where possible, the historical circumstances in which the material was spoken will be identified.

Kings During Jeremiah's Ministry
627–580 B.C.

Name of King	Reign Begins
Josiah	640 B.C.
Jehoahaz	609 B.C.
Jehoiakim	609 B.C.
Jehoiachin	598 B.C.
Zedekiah	597 B.C.
Gedaliah (governor)	587 B.C.

Jeremiah 1

Introduction to These Chapters

Chapter 1 introduces Jeremiah and establishes his
authority as a prophet. We are told where he comes from,
how long his ministry lasts, and how God calls him. The
chapter closes with two vision reports that further
explain Jeremiah's prophetic duties. Here is an outline of
the chapter.

   I. Introduction (1:1-3)
  II. Jeremiah's Call to Prophesy (1:4-10)
 III. Vision of a Rod of Almond (1:11-12)
 IV. Vision of a Boiling Pot (1:13-19)

Introduction (1:1-3)

These verses introduce us to the man Jeremiah and to
this collection of his prophecies. This introduction was
added to the written record of Jeremiah's prophecy
during its collection.

Jeremiah comes from a priestly family. His father,
hometown, and home territory are identified. (See
Glossary for details.)

Jeremiah first received the word of the Lord in the
thirteenth year of the reign of King Josiah. This is the year
627 B.C. Jehoiakim was king of Judah from 609–598 B.C.
Zedekiah was king of Judah from 598–587 B.C. The fifth
month is the Hebrew month of Ab, our July/August. The
Hebrew calendar begins the year in the spring,
approximately in our March/April.

13

The dates in Jeremiah 1:2-3 indicate that Jeremiah's prophecy ends with the fall of Jerusalem to the Babylonians in August of 587 B.C. The book, however, records Jeremiah's activities and prophecies until about 580 B.C. (chapters 40–44), after he is forced into exile in Egypt. So, this introduction to Jeremiah may at one time have stood at the beginning of a shorter collection of Jeremiah's words. This shorter collection could have been the present chapters 1–39.

Jeremiah's Call to Prophesy (1:4-10)

These verses record a conversation between God and Jeremiah in which God calls Jeremiah (verses 4-5), God gives Jeremiah his commission (verses 7-8), and God ordains Jeremiah to his duty as a prophet (verses 9-10), after overcoming Jeremiah's objections (verse 6).

The Old Testament writers realized that it was important for Jeremiah's readers, as it was for his listeners, to understand that Jeremiah's words come from God. The phrase the word of the Lord is a characteristic expression in Jeremiah. This phrase emphasizes that Jeremiah's words have authority because they are from God.

Old Testament Prophetic Speech

The Old Testament tells us in Genesis 1 that the word of God has creative power. According to Old Testament tradition, this creative power extends to God's word spoken by the prophet. The prophetic word about the future is not spoken to speculate about or to predict the future, but to make known God's word for the future. The prophet tells his listeners of God's intentions, and his words set in motion the process of carrying out those intentions. *The prophetic word acts to make things happen.*

The Israelites believed that oracles and demonstrations of God's words possessed a power that set in motion the accomplishment of God's word. Language was seen as a dynamic force that could affect the physical world. Thus, the prophetic future begins with the spoken word of the prophet.

This idea is one of the reasons that those people who opposed Jeremiah's prophecy took such harsh actions against him (Jeremiah 20:10; 37:15)). They considered his words treasonous at times, but they also recognized the creative power traditionally given to prophetic speech. Even his enemies granted some power to Jeremiah's message. They wanted Jeremiah to be quiet!

Jeremiah will not destroy and overthrow by brute force; nor will he alone build and plant (1:10). God's words in his mouth will accomplish these things. God touches Jeremiah's mouth as a seal and symbol of that task and that power.

Vision of a Rod of Almond (1:11-12)

Jeremiah has a vision (verse 11) and God interprets this vision (verse 12). Jeremiah sees the branch of an almond tree. God explains that this is a sign of God's watchful care over the words that Jeremiah must speak.

The Hebrew text in these two verses has a play on words which does not come across in the English translation. The Hebrew word for almond (shaqed) is nearly the same as the word for watchful (shoqed).

God is a watchman who appoints prophets as watchmen (see Jeremiah 6:17; Ezekiel 3:17) to warn to the Isarelite people of their danger. The watchman of a city has the responsibility for raising an alarm should an enemy approach. Failure to raise the alarm is a serious offense because innocent lives could be lost.

Almond trees are cultivated in Palestine and are among the first fruits to blossom (wake) in the spring. They are presented as a reminder for Jeremiah. He may take courage from the sight of these trees and be reminded of God's watchful care and power.

Vision of a Boiling Pot (1:13-19)

God shows Jeremiah a boiling pot (verse 13), explains its meaning (verses 14-16), and tells what this will mean for the prophet (verses 17-19).

The boiling pot (possibly a wide-mouthed cooking pot) symbolizes conquerors who will enter Judah from the north. (The Assyrians also came into Israel from the north. Egypt is referred to as the *South* elsewhere in the Old Testament.)

That the pot is facing away from the north implies that it is spilling its hot contents (warfare) into Judah. God will call forth the invaders as agents of punishment. Though the foe is not named, it is most likely Babylon. Babylonian forces moved northwest through Syria, then turned south, through northern Israel, and moved into Judah in their military campaigns of 605 B.C. and 597 B.C.

The reasons for the coming invasion are given in verse 16. The people of Israel have turned their backs on the covenant and taken up the worship of foreign gods.

No date is attached to this vision. It may have come, however, near the time of Jeremiah's call to prophesy (627 B.C.) during the reign of King Josiah (640–609 B.C.). Josiah's father, King Manasseh, had encouraged the worship of foreign gods in Israel. Josiah tried to get rid of these idolatrous practices and return Israel to the true worship of God. Jeremiah's vision confirms the need for such reform. The consequence Judah must face for idolatry and wickedness will be occupation of the land by foreigners. A major theme throughout Jeremiah's prophecy is that God punishes those who forsake the covenant and who worship other gods.

God warns Jeremiah that he must speak as God commands. If Jeremiah *breaks down* (NRSV, NIV = *be terrified*) in the face of opposition to his message, God will *break* him down.

God uses images of strength in time of war (verse 18) to convince Jeremiah that he can survive the attacks of those who will oppose him. The opposition will come from all quarters of life in Israel—from the kings, from government officials, from the clergy, and from the common people. Jeremiah is forewarned but also forearmed. God will strengthen and save him.

The first chapter ends on both a note of warning and a note of encouragement. We see that Jeremiah is wise to realize the consequences of God's call and to, at first, protest his call. Jeremiah's message, to Israel and to other nations, will grieve him and put him in danger.

§ § § § § § §

The Message of Jeremiah 1

In chapter 1, Jeremiah is introduced, called, commissioned, strengthened, and sent out to speak God's word. This sets the stage for the rest of the book. What does this chapter tell us about the ministry of a prophet?

§ Prophets speak at God's direction within specific historical situations. Their words are related to life (and death) issues and are not just theoretical.

§ God calls even those who feel unprepared.

§ This call is not to be taken lightly. The prophet must expect personal opposition and opposition to his prophecy.

§ The prophetic word is a creative force because it is God's word.

§ God prepares the prophet for the prophetic task and watches over the prophet's life.

§ § § § § § §

Jeremiah 2–4

Introduction to These Chapters

These chapters contain oracles against Israel that list Israel's sins and announce the punishment to come. In the middle of these announcements of judgment are oracles calling for repentance and return to the blessings of the Lord. Prophets did not usually deliver long, prepared sermons. Rather, they spoke brief messages as the occasion and word of God demanded.

The oracles from Jeremiah 2 through Jeremiah 6 are probably from the time of the reign of King Josiah (640–609 B.C.).

Here is an outline of chapters 2–4:

I. Oracles Against Unfaithful Israel (2:1-37)
   A. When Israel was devoted to God (2:1-3)
   B. God's faithfulness (2:4-13)
   C. Israel a slave of foreigners (2:14-19)
   D. Israel degenerate and shamed (2:20-28)
   E. Israel rejected God's correction (2:29-37)
II. Oracles Calling Israel to Repent (3:1-4:4)
   A. Israel called from her harlotry (3:1-5)
   B. Judah called to acknowledge her guilt (3:6-20)
   C. Israel must admit her shame (3:21-4:4)
III. Oracles About the Foe from the North (4:5-31)
   A. The alarm raised in Judah (4:5-10)
   B. Armies will sweep over Jerusalem (4:11-18)
   C. Jeremiah laments the disaster (4:19-22)
   D. Vision of the Desolation to Come (4:23-31)

When Israel Was Devoted to God (2:1-3)

In verses 1-3, God speaks of Israel as a bride. The *devotion of your youth* in the wilderness refers to the Sinai covenant and to the time of Israel's wandering in the wilderness. The covenant is compared to the marriage vow in which Israel was once faithful. Israel is also compared to the *first fruits* of harvest, the choicest of God's crop. Israel is *holy,* that is, set apart and chosen by God.

Those who ate (NRSV; NIV = *devour*) are Israel's enemies (for example, the Canaanites and the Philistines) against whom God offered protection.

By using the metaphors of the bride and fruits, God recalls a better time in Israel's past.

God's Faithfulness (2:4-13)

These verses are a prophetic announcement of judgment. Many such announcements are found in Jeremiah and in other prophetic books (for example, in Ezekiel and Amos). An oracle is the revealed word of God. The prophet is God's messenger, reporting the word to the people. In general, such oracles have three parts:
1. an introduction or call to attention
2. a description of sins
3. a proclamation of punishment

Not all oracles of judgment have all three parts. Some have all the parts but in a different order.

Judgment is announced because of specific failures on the part of the people. The listing of these failures shows that God's judgment is rational and just.

These messenger speeches often begin with the phrase *Hear the word of the LORD* or *Thus says the LORD.* They often end with *says the LORD* or *declares the LORD.* These phrases alert the listeners, and the readers, to the authority of the prophet's words.

Be aware of these parts of prophetic speech as you read Jeremiah's prophecies. In verses 4-13 they are:
(1) the call to attention—verse 4, *Hear . . .*

(2) the description of sin—verses 5-8, 10-13, *Thus says the* LORD . . .

(3) the proclamation of punishment—verse 9, *Therefore* . . .

Notice in this chapter how Jerusalem, house of Jacob, and families of Israel are all used to identify God's people. Israel and Judah are sometimes used in Jeremiah to mean specifically the northern and southern kingdoms respectively. Often, however, Jeremiah uses these names interchangeably to mean all the chosen people.

God reminds Israel of what was done for her in the past (verses 5-7*a*). Once in the Promised Land, however, Israel strayed to other gods (verses 7*b*-8).

The *wilderness* (verse 6, also in Jeremiah 23:10) is an area to the south and east of Judah where there was not enough rainfall for farming. In the spring, following the winter rains, there are pastures here. Pits or cisterns are dug to catch and hold rainwater.

The failures of the priests and the guardians of the teachings of the law may point to a time during King Josiah's reform efforts. The reform (described in 2 Kings 23:4-28) probably focused on external changes, while the heart of the people still *went after things that do not profit* (NRSV; NIV = *for worthless idols*). Jeremiah probably supported Josiah's reform, though it is doubtful that he had an official role in it. He became disillusioned with the reform program even before Josiah's death (Jeremiah 3:10; 6:16-21). False prophecy and unfaithful leaders continue to be a problem after Josiah's death (Jeremiah 23:16-22).

God calls heaven to witness Israel's evil. The people have abandoned the living God for lifeless idols *(cisterns that can hold no water)*. They have become as worthless as the idols they worship.

Israel a Slave of Foreigners (2:14-19)

Israel has abandoned her covenant birthright of responsible freedom to become a slave of Assyria *(lions) and Egypt (Memphis and Tahpanhes)*. This oracle refers to the political and military intrigue that accompanied the decline of Assyrian power. Both Egypt and Babylon were eager to assert themselves. Josiah's religious reforms were a repudiation of Assyrian gods and a declaration of independence from Assyrian domination. Josiah was killed in battle trying to keep Egypt and Assyria from joining forces against Babylon and taking control of Judah. After Josiah's death in 609 B.C., Judah was under Egyptian control until 605 B.C. when the Babylonians defeated the Egyptians at the Battle of Carchemish.

Israel Degenerate and Shamed (2:20-28)

In many prophetic oracles a nation, city, or group of people is personified and addressed as a single person. In this oracle, sinful Israel is compared to a stubborn ox (verse 20), a harlot (verse 20), a wild vine (verse 21), a lustful animal (verses 22-24), and a thief (verse 26). Israel denies her guilt, despite the evidence of her idol worship and human sacrifice (verse 23). Jeremiah mocks those who look to trees and stones, which are the objects of pagan worship, as if they were the living God. Sarcastically, he asks the people how handmade gods can save them.

Israel Rejected God's Correction (2:29-37)

Israel cannot claim to be ignorant (verse 29) or guiltless (verse 35) of her sins. More of Israel's sins are listed. She has not listened to God's word but has killed prophets and forgotten the covenant. She has taught her wicked ways to other nations (verse 33). Lawlessness, perhaps motivated by greed, has resulted in the death of the poor, even those who were not breaking in to steal something.

Your hands on your head is a sign of the sorrow and shame Israel will face.

Chapter 2 closes with Israel alone and condemned.

Israel Called from Her Harlotry (3:1-5)

Jeremiah uses an example from the Law (Deueteronomy 24:1-4) to witness to Israel's dilemma. In the covenant or marriage contract (Jeremiah 2:1-3), God is the husband and Israel the wife. But Israel is an indecent wife, prostituting itself with other gods (see also Hosea 3:1-5). The metaphor of the unfaithful wife turned harlot dramatically portrays Israel's idol worship. This is more than a metaphor, however. Some fertility cults practiced cult prostitution as a means of acting out the regeneration of the earth each year.

Ironically, it is because of the so-called fertility rites that God withholds life-giving rain from the land. This is a witness to Israel's sin, but she still does evil.

Judah Called to Acknowledge Her Guilt (3:6-20)

In this oracle Israel and Judah refer to the northern and southern kingdoms. Judah fails to learn from Israel's mistakes and follows her sister into idol worship. Because of this, Judah will follow Israel into exile (*a decree of divorce,* verse 8). As in previous oracles, the metaphors are mixed. Israel is both a faithless wife and faithless *children* (verse 14 NRSV; NIV = *people*).

God's intentions, however, are for deliverance. In mercy, God maintains steadfast love for Israel (verse 12). Israel and Judah will be drawn from exile *(the north)* and reunited under faithful rulers *(shepherds,* verse 15). More than this, God envisions a day when all nations will gather in peace in Jerusalem. Jerusalem will replace the ark as the symbol of the throne of God.

Verses 19-20 continue the thought of verses 1-5. Israel is addressed as a daughter to whom God wants to bequeath land.

Israel Must Admit Her Shame (3:21-4:4)

From the heights, or high places where pagan worship is held, Israel (now called a son) must confess and repent.

The *shameful thing* (NRSV) or "shameful gods" (NIV) mentioned in verse 24 refers to Israel's idol worship.

The conditions of repentance (4:1-4) are the removal of

pagan shrines (verse 1), professing the worship of the Lord (verse 2), and having the mark of the Lord on their hearts, not just as a physical sign such as circumcision.

An oath (*if you swear*, verse 2) is very powerful. It affirms the existence of the god named and calls on the god's power. Israel was swearing by, and thus affirming, other gods.

The promise that Israel can again be a source of blessing and praise to other nations reflects the promise of Jeremiah 3:17.

The Alarm Raised in Judah (4:5-10)

Trumpets and cries will signal the approach of the enemy from the north.

That day (verse 9) is similar in impact to the *day of the* LORD spoken of by Amos (for example, Amos 5:18). The Israelites had traditionally expected the day of the Lord to be a day in which their enemies would be crushed. Jeremiah and Amos, however, proclaim it as a day of defeat for Israel.

Jeremiah objects to God about this proclamation (verse 10). In this case, he may be voicing questions other Israelites are asking. Instead of being open to a new word from God, they cling to God's promises from the past while continuing to sin. These past promises had been hardened into a kind of national theology.

This national theology was grounded on God's choice of Zion as God's earthly dwelling, on the promise of an eternal Davidic kingship, and on the promises of victory over enemies that had been given by prophets years before. The people ignored the moral spiritual obligations that went with these promises, however (Jeremiah 7:8-10).

Even as the people were proudly confident that God would never destroy Jerusalem, they complained in alarm at the danger they saw on their doorstep.

Armies Will Sweep over Jerusalem (4:11-18)

The enemy comes as a hot desert wind with superhuman powers of destruction. The alarm is announced from Dan (in the north) to Mount Ephraim (in central Palestine).

Jeremiah Laments the Disasters (4:19-22)

In verses 19-22, Jeremiah laments the disaster coming upon his people. He knows they are guilty, but he is in anguish over their fate. Jeremiah feels deeply for his people and takes no joy in their downfall.

Tents (verse 20) is a reference to *home*. The curtains divide the tent into eating and sleeping areas. Long after Israel left her nomadic tents for permanent houses, the nomadic days were remembered.

Vision of the Desolation to Come (4:23-31)

Jeremiah sees the earth laid waste and void as it was before creation (Genesis 1:2; 2:5). In Jeremiah's vision, the earth, the heavens, and the people feel the force of God's judgment. Verse 27 softens the judgment and indicates that this is not the cataclysmic end of the age. The earth and some of God's people will survive the devastation. Instead of being a blessing, Israel has brought desolation to the earth.

Egyptian women used mineral compounds, typically colored black or green, to paint around their eyes. The three biblical references to eye paint associate it with women of bad reputation (verse 30; 2 Kings 9:30; Ezekiel 23:40).

Lovers (verse 30) are the nations whose gods Israel worshiped. *Daughter of Zion* (verse 31) is a reference to Jerusalem.

§ § § § § § § §

The Message of Jeremiah 2-4

Even during the time of national religious reform by King Josiah, Jeremiah has much to say against the ways of his people. He holds their present idolatry and disobedience up to the light of the past. Their past relationship with God could show them the way into a blessed future. Their present ways could only lead to destruction for Israel and for the earth.

What must the people of Israel do to gain new life in the Lord?

§ Remember the past: God's saving actions and the promises which God and Israel made to one another in the wildnerness.

§ Confess their sins of idolatry and wickedness.

§ Return to the covenant relationship in "truth, justice and righteousness," not just in ritual.

§ § § § § § §

Jeremiah 5–7

Introduction to These Chapters

Chapters 5 and 6 contain oracles announcing the corruptions for which Israel is judged. Chapter 7 begins with a sermon that Jeremiah preaches in the Temple in Jerusalem. The last half of the chapter lists abuses in worship of which the people are guilty. Here is an outline of these chapters:

I. The Search for Truth and Justice in Israel Is Futile (5:1-31)
   A. Jeremiah is to search for a faithful man (5:1-6)
   B. God has no choice but to judge (5:7-11)
   C. Consequences of ignoring God's word (5:12-17)
   D. A word of hope (5:18-19)
   E. The foolish do not fear the Lord (5:20-31)
II. The Foe from the North Approaches (6:1-30)
   A. Oracles of war against Jerusalem (6:1-8)
   B. No one will listen to the word of God (6:9-12)
   C. The people sin (6:13-21)
   D. The foe from the north strikes terror (6:22-26)
   E. Jeremiah to test God's people (6:27-30)
III. Oracles Concerning the Temple (7:1-8:3)
   A. Jeremiah's Temple sermon (7:1-15)
   B. Oracle against idolatrous worship (7:16-8:3)

Jeremiah Is to Search for a Faithful Man (5:1-6)

At God's command, Jeremiah searches in Jerusalem for someone on whom God can base a pardon for Israel (verses 1-2; see also Genesis 18:23-33). Jeremiah looks, but he reports that he finds no one, either among the poor or the privileged, who will repent.

The prophetic *therefore* is declared (verse 6)—enemies will devour them. The prophetic *therefore* is announced in the manner of a judgment in a legal case. Judgment is not announced without evidence nor by the whim of the judge. The case is based on the people's failure to live up to their obligations in the covenant they made with God. These obligations include actions that are directed by the knowledge of God. To know God is more than mental affirmation. This knowledge involves being in right relationship to God and to others.

God Has No Choice but to Judge (5:7-11)

In the face of Israel's idolatry and immorality, God has no choice but to announce judgment.

Jeremiah again uses the metaphor of the vine for Israel (see also Jeremiah 2:21).

Notice the note of hope—*do not make a full end* (NRSV; NIV = *do not destroy them completely*). Some of the people will be saved because God's long-term purpose is Israel's redemption.

Consequences of Ignoring God's Word (5:12-17)

In this oracle, Jeremiah throws the people's blasphemy back at them by quoting their own arrogant words. The people ignored the prophetic word as mere wind, not believing it as God's word. Because of this, Jeremiah's prophetic word will be as fire and the people as firewood. This is a vivid illustration of the dynamic and creative power of prophetic speech. It is not that Jeremiah's words will cause the people to burst into flame. Rather, his words set into motion the accomplishment of God's will as surely as fire consumes wood.

The *ancient* and *enduring nation* (verse 15) is probably Babylon. Even in the best of times, the average Israelite did not live far above subsistence level. The threat of hunger was always close. A crop failure or a war could bring starvation. Jeremiah warns that Israel's children will be killed and the survivors will face starvation (verse 17).

A Word of Hope (5:18-19)

The *day of the* LORD will not destroy all of Israel. Some of God's people will survive so that they may question what has happened to them. In exile, the people will seek the meaning of their fate, and God will provide answers to them through the prophetic word.

After the first group of exiles was taken to Babylon in 597 B.C., Jeremiah wrote them a letter (Jeremiah 29:1-23). This letter advised them on how to live in exile and how to understand God's plan for them.

The Foolish Do Not Fear the Lord (5:20-31)

Judah forgets that *fear of the* LORD *is the beginning of knowledge* (Proverbs 1:7). The people close their eyes to the evidence of God's greatness. They tolerate injustice and ignore their duties to the defenseless (Deuteronomy 24:17-18; Amos 2:6-7).

Jeremiah's impassioned speech switches from second person *(you)* to third person *(they)* and back again. *You* and *they* are the people of Israel. Sometimes it is also difficult to tell where one speech ends and another begins.

In verse 24, Jeremiah again uses imagery from Israel's agricultural life. The autumn rain is the early rain of October and November. This rain softens the ground for cultivation. The latter, or spring rains in April and May end the rainy season and begin the harvest season. Hot winds then come off the desert bringing the heat and dyness of summer. The *weeks for harvest* are the weeks after the spring rains are over when rain would spoil the crop.

False leadership (verses 30-31) is a recurring reason for judgment (Jeremiah 6:13-15; 8:11-12; 23:9-22).

The Foe from the North Approaches (6:1-30)

This chapter opens with a call for the alarms of war to be sounded close to Jerusalem.

Oracle of War Against Jerusalem (6:1-8)

Jerusalem, the once lovely daughter of God, will be destroyed by kings and their armies *(shepherds with their flocks)*. The pastoral image of shepherds and flocks is turned against Jerusalem as the battle plans are laid. The siege has not yet come, however. This oracle is a warning that may yet avert disaster.

Jeremiah may have delivered this oracle before the Babylonian siege against Jerusalem in 598 B.C.

No One Will Listen to the Word of God (6:9-12)

God commissions Jeremiah to search for and gather any good fruit out of the people of Israel (as in Jeremiah 5:1).

In verses 10-11, Jeremiah voices frustration and despair that his message is ignored. Though he would rather not speak words of judgment, he cannot hold back (see also Jeremiah 20:9). Having been prophesying for perhaps fifteen to twenty years by this time, Jeremiah is weary.

The People Sin (6:13-21)

Two oracles condemn the prophets and priests (verses 13-15) and the people (verses 16-21).

The first oracle lists three areas of wickedness—greed and dishonesty prevail in daily life (verse 13; also Jeremiah 8:10), leaders promise material and spiritual well-being to the dishonest (verse 14), and the people are not ashamed of their idolatry and immorality (verse 15).

The second oracle reminds the people of Israel of the chances they had to know and to do God's will. The *ancient paths* are the covenant. The *watchmen* (NIV, NRSV = *sentinels*) are the prophets. Israel rejected the covenant, the prophets, and the law in favor of empty ritual (verse 20). Jeremiah declares that the finest and rarest offerings are no substitute for walking in the way of the Lord. A *stumbling block* (NRSV; NIV = *obstacles*) is a source of failure (verse 21). Because the people have ignored God's law and God's prophets, stumbling blocks, or obstacles, will be set before them. Elsewhere in the Old Testament, idols are called stumbling blocks. (See for example, Ezekiel 7:19.)

The Foe from the North Strikes Terror (6:22-26)

The voice of God (verses 22-23) and the voice of the people (verses 24-26) are heard as the destroyer draws near. *Terror on every side* is used elsewhere in Jeremiah to express overwhelming danger (Jeremiah 20:3, 10; 46:5; 49:29). Normal life will cease. The people will be in pain—not the pain of birth but that of mourning.

Jeremiah to Test God's People (6:27-30)

Chapter 6 closes with a charge to Jeremiah to analyze and test the people to see if any faithfulness may be found in them. Here we see another in Jeremiah's rich store of metaphors. In the refining process, metal is heated to remove the slag. It is then reheated into a liquid in a clay, cup-shaped container over a charcoal fire to further purify it. Air forced through bellows raises the temperature of the fire so that impurities are removed and the metal is consolidated. Silver is obtained by refining silver-rich lead ore.

Nothing of value is to be found in Israel, only base and refuse metal. The refining trials Israel has endured have not purified her of her wickedness.

This commission comes at the end of a group of oracles that are generally from the time of King Josiah (Jeremiah 1–6). The oracles beginning in chapter 7 and continuing through chapter 20 are, for the most part, from the reign of King Jehoiakim (609–598 B.C.).

Oracles Concerning the Temple (7:1-8:3)

In the gate of the Temple in Jerusalem, Jeremiah preaches a sermon against false trust in external religion (verses 1-15). The rest of the chapter expands on points of the sermon (7:16-8:3).

Jeremiah's Temple Sermon (7:1-15)

From 609–605 B.C., after Josiah's death at Megiddo, Judah remained under Egyptian domination. King Jehoahaz was taken to Egypt and his brother Jehoiakim put on the throne. Babylon was not yet ready to move against Judah. Under Jehoiakim, Josiah's reform effort lapsed. Early in his reign, Jehoiakim built a new palace using forced labor, despite the heavy taxation imposed by Egypt. Pagan worship practices resumed and public morality declined.

Staggered by the blow of Josiah's death, Israel retreated into the past. The people clung to the notion that the city, the Temple, and the nation were eternally secure. In this atmosphere, Jeremiah stands in the Temple (probably in one of the gates separating the inner and outer courts of the Temple) and declares that this trust in the past is a deception.

Jeremiah confronts the people with their hypocrisy and self-deception. He tells them to go to Shiloh to see the tangible evidence that a sanctuary could be destroyed. Shiloh was the site of an important sanctuary in ancient Israel during the time of Samuel. The Old Testament does not tell of its destruction, but archaeological excavations indicate that it was destroyed around 1050 B.C., probably by the Philistines when they captured the ark of the covenant (1 Samuel 4:11).

Jeremiah confirms that God lent the divine presence (*my name*) to the Temple and gave the land to the people of Israel. But the Israelites (*offspring* or *people of Ephraim*) have revoked the agreement by their wickedness.

Immediately after delivering this sermon, Jeremiah is arrested and put on trial. But he is released after some high government officials defend him (Jeremiah 26).

Oracle Against Idolatrous Worship (7:16–8:3)

God forbids Jeremiah to intercede for the people even though this is part of Jeremiah's duty as a prophet. (See also Jeremiah 11:14; 15:1.)

The *queen of heaven* is, perhaps, the goddess Ishtar (see also Jeremiah 44:15-28).

Verses 21-28 continue the charges and commands concerning false worship. This sermon may also have been delivered in the Temple, though at a different time from verses 1-15.

The *burnt offerings* are entirely burned on the altar, but other types of sacrifice are eaten in part by the worshipers. Jeremiah says that the people might as well eat it all because the sacrifices are mere flesh.

Verses 22-23 may refer to the Ten Commandments, where moral instead of ceremonial law is given.

In verse 29 Jeremiah is commanded to cut his hair and raise a funeral lament, both of which are part of the ritual of mourning. This symbolic act, on the very heights where Judah offered sacrifices to idols, shows that Judah is as good as dead because of sin (7:30–8:3).

The people defile the Temple with pagan idols. Worst of all, they offer human sacrifices on pagan altars, though this is strictly forbidden in the Law (Leviticus 18:21).

Marriage feasts are traditionally the scene of singing, dancing, and the reciting of love poems. But Judah will no longer celebrate the joy of new families being formed (verse 34). Those of God's people who survive the Exile (Jeremiah 8:3) will wish for death.

§ § § § § § §

The Message of Jeremiah 5–7

Judment is announced on Israel for specific reasons. The people of Israel have known what is expected of them all along. God has not just suddenly changed the Law. Jeremiah proclaims that Israel must count on God's justice as well as on God's blessing.

On what foundation are Jeremiah's announcements of judgment against Israel based?

§ Israel has failed to live up to its part of the relationship.

§ The people take God's presence with them for granted even as they turn away from righteousness.

§ Their lives are not directed by knowledge of God or of God's will.

§ Truth, justice, and righteousness are lacking in Israel. Therefore, God is justiified in punishing Israel.

§ § § § § § §

Jeremiah 8–10

Introduction to These Chapters

The first three verses of chapter 8 conclude the oracle that begins in Jeremiah 7:29. Chapters 8:4–10:25 are a collection of prophetic oracles, laments, and prayers that were probably delivered during the reign of King Jehoiakim (609–598 B.C.). Here is an outline of the content of these chapters:

I. Oracles Against Israel and a Lament for Her Fate (8:4-9:1)
   A. The unnaturalness of sin (8:4-12)
   B. God and Israel are disappointed (8:13-17)
   C. The people's sickness (8:18-9:1)
II. Lamentations Over the People of Israel (9:2-26)
   A. Justice demands punishment for sins (9:2-9)
   B. Lament and interpretation (9:10-16)
   C. Funeral lament for Zion (9:17-22)
   D. The mark of those who know God (9:23-26)
III. Oracles Against Idols and a Plea for Mercy (10:1-25)
   A. Comparing lifeless idols to God (10:1-16)
   B. Oracle to those living under siege (10:17-22)
   C. Prayer for mercy (10:23-25)

The Unnaturalness of Sin (8:4-12)

This oracle begins with a series of rhetorical, common-sense type questions and comparisons (see also Jeremiah 18:14-16). If a man falls, does he not naturally get up as quickly as possible? Is Israel to do less than even the birds, who follow their natural instincts? But Israel has rejected both the written word (the Law) and the spoken word (the prophet) of God.

Verses 8 and 9 refer to wise men and scribes, who are advisors to the king, and to officials of the royal court.

Israel is unashamed, unable even to blush. The people have reversed the order God established for them. Now they worship idols, they cheat one another, they offer false promises of peace, and they seek their own wisdom.

Elsewhere Jeremiah points to this reversal of the established order—the ox has broken its yoke (2:20), the cultivated vine has become a wild vine (2:21), priests and prophets lie (5:31). In the face of Israel's rebellion, Jeremiah proclaims that true freedom and well-being lie in obedience to God, not in breaking away.

Verses 10-12 are the same as Jeremiah 6:12-15.

God and Israel Are Disappointed (8:13-17)·

This oracle continues the theme of a reversal of natural or expected circumstances.

God expects good fruit from the people of Israel, but they have produced none. *What I gave* or *have given them* (verse 13) is perhaps the word of God proclaimed through the Law and the prophets.

The people expect physical, material, and spiritual well-being but find only death. Their fortified cities are no refuge from the consequences of sin. They must drink the cup of God's wrath (see also Jeremiah 9:15). This cup is a symbol not of refreshment but of punishment.

The foe from the north is heard from Dan, the northernmost point in Israel (verse 16). Jeremiah pictures the enemy in terms of war horses and snakes, against which Israel will have no defense.

The People's Sickness (8:18-9:1)

The disruption in the proper relationship between God and the people of Israel results in sickness and death. The circumstances described in the previous two oracles throw Jeremiah into the depths of mourning for his people. He cries out in despair for healing.

We cannot tell from the context of this lament the exact date or circumstances in which it was spoken. It probably comes from the reign of King Jehoiakim at a time when Jeremiah sees Israel moving farther away from God and closer to destruction. During the years of his prophecy, Jeremiah must have been, at times, under great physical, spiritual, and emotional stress. At such a time, he may have wept and cried aloud this lament.

The word *balm* (verse 22) indicates an aromatic, resinous discharge taken from various trees and shrubs and made into a healing salve. Resins do not decay and are antiseptic, though some are more effective than others in stopping the bacterial infections that are found in wounds. The *balm of Gilead* may be made from a tree grown in the part of Gilead which is in the tropical regions of the Jordan Valley.

Notice that the people of Israel are portrayed as both wounded but alive (verses 19-21) and as slain (9:1). In prophetic speech tenses and times are often mixed. The future is spoken of as if it is the present so that the presnt and future somehow exist together. This way of speaking is an expression of the creative power credited to the prophetic word.

Justic Demands Punishment for Sins (9:2-9)

In contrast to the lament in Jeremiah 8:18–9:1, Jeremiah grieves over the complete corruption of the people and would like to be able to escape his duties to them (verse 2). He has contempt for their deceit and oppression of one another.

Jeremiah must have had not only moments of weariness and despair but also moments of anger over Israel's refusal to hear and obey God's word.

The justice of God, which Israel knows well, demands

punishment for the people's sins. This stress on the justice of God's case against Israel is an important element in Jeremiah's prophecy. Even though God's justice demands punishment, the people may yet rely on this justice to guide them in the future. By recognizing the reasons for their tragedy, the people of Israel can find their way back to God.

Lament and Interpretation (9:10-16)

Jeremiah laments ruined Judah. The land is empty of the beasts that should live there, and the cities are empty of people. The stillness of death lies over everything. Again, Jeremiah presents a picture of the reversal of the natural order of life. He voices questions the people may ask about what is happening to them (verse 12). God explains the reasons for the desolation (verses 13-16).

In 598 B.C. and 582 B.C. the Babylonians deported large numbers of Israelites. After the siege in 587 B.C., the city of Jerusalem was little more than a heap of ruins. After the deportations of 582 B.C., Judah was practically desolate of inhabitants. The killing, starvation, and deportation left only a relatively small number of peasants in the land.

During the siege of 588–587 B.C., food was scarce and the people were reduced to eating *wormwood* (NRSV; NIV = *bitter food) and poison water* (see also Ezekiel 4:9-17). Merchants were selling terrible food at exoribant prices.

Funeral Lament for Zion (9:17-22)

These verses pick up the theme of mourning introduced in verse 10. This is a funeral lament for Zion. Mourning is carried out as it would be for a beloved person who has died. (See also Jeremiah 16:5-9.) Jeremiah is forbidden the traditional expressions of mourning.

Professional mourning women are hired to bewail the people's fate. The mourners utter shrill cries or wails, beat their breasts, and perhaps cut or pull out some of their hair. The ritual may also include the wearing of sackcloth (a garment made of camel or goat hair), tearing of garments, scattering dirt or ashes on the head, lying in the dirt, wailing and weeping, and lacerating the body. Songs and poems of mourning are composed and either recited or sung.

The Mark of Those Who Know God (9:23-26)

Verses 23-24 are a kind of wisdom oracle. God contrasts the common goals of humankind, such as power and riches, with the only truly worthy goal, which is knowledge of God. Again, a contrast is offered between the misguided practices of the people and the practices ordained by God. Israel's only proper boast and source of pride are in God's righteous deeds. Knowledge of God's ways will lead to blessing (see also Jeremiah 7:5-7, 23). This knowledge is not just intellectual but is to be put into practice.

Verses 25-26 shift focus to include foreigners as well as Israelites. A contrast is offered between outward form and inward being. Cicumcision (in addition to ritual and sacrifice) has little value unless it indicates a right relationship to God (see also Jeremiah 4:4).

The practice of circumcision among the Arabs is implied because Ishmael, their ancestor, was circumcised by Abraham (see Genesis 17:23). Circumcision was also practiced in Egypt. Circumcision is not required in the Ten Commandments. It came to be regarded as a requirement for inclusion in the community of Israel after the Israelites developed a strong national awareness. It also came to be seen as an outward sign of the covenant between God and Israel.

Chapter 9 ends with instructions from God for what is required of Israel. Israel must give up her pride and self-glorification. If pride is the ground of sin, then love and justice are the basis of a right relationship with God.

Comparing Lifeless Idols to God (10:1-16)

The oracle contrasts worthless heathen idols made of wood and metal, which are the products of human labor, with the living God of Israel, who is the creator of the world and Israel's redeemer.

The *signs* (verse 2) are eclipses and comets or other unusual celestial occurrences taken as important signs in ancient astrology. The worship of heavenly bodies and the practice of astrology are considered idolatrous. King Manasseh (687-642 B.C.) may have introduced star worship into Israel (2 Kings 21:5).

Verses 12-16 are also found in Jeremiah 51:15-19. This is an oracle against Babylon.

Clothing of violet and purple (verse 9) is expensive and precious. The purple dye is produced from the murex shell found along the Phoenician coast.

In Jeremiah 9:25-26, Israel is listed among the heathen who are *uncircumcised in heart*. This oracle in 10:1-16 emphasizes the foolishness and obvious error of trusting in heathen idols. Israel has nothing to gain by imitating her neighbors.

Oracle to Those Living Under Siege (10:17-22)

This oracle continues the thought of 9:10-22 but at a later time, perhaps during the siege of 598 B.C. The passage is a dialogue between Jeremiah (verses 17-18, 22) and Jerusalem (verses 19-21). The city is personified as a mother who is thrown out of her home (*tent*, verse 20) and who loses her children. She is to gather her belongings in a bundle and prepare to leave her homeland.

The *shepherds* (verse 21) are Israel's leaders. The *commotion from the land of the north* refers to the Babylonians.

Prayer for Mercy (10:23-25)

In verses 23-24 Jeremiah prays for himself and perhaps also for Judah. He confesses his, and the people's, guilt.

He admits that human beings need God's guidance, justice, and mercy.

Verse 25 speaks of the desolation of Judah as an accomplished fact. Its perspective is one of death and of the need for revenge. This verse is also found in Psalm 79:6-7.

§ § § § § § §

The Message of Jeremiah 8-10

The prophecies and prayers of chapters 8-10 warn that those who ignore God's instruction (for example, 8:9) are doomed to lose their way in sin (see 10:23).

What are God's instructions to Israel (see 9:23-26)?

§ Human knowledge, power, and wealth offer no real security nor cause for pride.

§ The goal of life should be to know and understand what God is like and what God requires.

§ Knowledge of God requires understanding and practice of God's will.

§ God practices steadfast love, justice, and righteousness and so must the people of God.

§ Physical symbols (such as circumcision) and ritual (such as worship) are empty without wholehearted commitment to God's will.

§ § § § § § §

Jeremiah 11–15

Introduction to These Chapters

This section contains laments, prayers, oracles, and a report of a sign act that Jeremiah is commanded to perform. The first two of Jeremiah's personal laments tell of Jeremiah's inner struggles with his prophetic office and the oppression he lives under.
Here is an outline of these chapters:

    I. Jeremiah and the Covenant (11:1-17)
    II. Jeremiah Laments His Fate (11:18–12:6)
    III. Lamentation for Judah (12:7-17)
        A. God laments Judah's fate (12:7-13)
        B. God offers hope for other nations (12:14-17)
    IV. Pride and Sin Bring Punishment (13:1-27)
        A. The sign of the linen waistcloth (13:1-11)
        B. A proverb is reinterpreted (13:12-14)
        C. A plea for repentance (13:15-17)
        D. Oracle against Jerusalem's shame (13:18-27)
    V. Lamentation over Judah (14:1–15:4)
        A. Lament and prayer because of drought (14:1-12)
        B. Oracle against false prophets (14:13-16)
        C. Lament, prayer, God's response (14:17–15:9)
    VI. Jeremiah's Second Personal Lament (15:10-21)

Jeremiah and the Covenant (11:1-17)

    God talks to Jeremiah about the legal basis for the punishment coming to Israel. This basis is the covenant that was sworn to by both God and Israel at Sinai.

In this oracle, the giving of the Law (Exodus 20:1-17) and the making of the covenant (Exodus 19:5; Deuteronomy 7:12) are to be seen within the context of God's redemptive actions for Israel. One of these redemptive acts was bringing the children of Israel out of bondage in Egypt (verse 4).

Because Israel and Judah broke God's commandments, God will apply the terms of the covenant to them. These terms include judgment for sin and for failure to abide by God's commandments (Exodus 34:6-7; Deuteronomy 7:9-10).

The *iron smelting* furnace (verse 4) is an image borrowed from the process of separating metal from ore. The ore is broken up into chunks that are then melted in a furnace. The metal then separates from the slag, or waste material. The liquid metal is cast into ingots to be carried to the smith's forge or shop.

Verses 9-13 tell of the conspiracy or revolt against the covenant by Israel and Judah. The situation described may be the time of King Jehoiakim, when the religious reforms of King Josiah were abandoned.

Because of their revolt, God again tells Jeremiah he cannot intercede for the people. As their rituals are useless, so will be Jeremiah's prayers for them.

Verses 15-16 are a poem to which the prose of verse 17 has been added. *My beloved* is Israel.

Jeremiah may have spoken this poem in the courts of the Temple where olive trees are planted (see also Psalm 52:8). The trees and the Temple were burned by the Babylonians in 587 B.C.

Jeremiah Laments His Fate (11:18-12:6)

Verses 18-21 tell of a plot against Jeremiah's life by certain men of Anathoth, some of whom are perhaps from his own family (see 12:6). Jeremiah may have identified some of them with false prophets and priests. The plot may have even originated among the priests and prophets of Jerusalem who wanted to silence Jeremiah after his preaching in the Temple (see Jeremiah 26:11).

Because he is the target of evil, Jeremiah complains to God and asks, *Why do the wicked* (NIV; NRSV = *guilty*) *prosper* (12:1)? This is the first time in the Old Testament that such a question is put to God. As if he is in a divine court, Jeremiah pleads his case to God. He questions the prevailing view that the wicked always suffer and the righteous always prosper. His experience had shown him that the wicked, faithful on the surface at least, do prosper.

Jeremiah approaches God confident of his own integrity. His belief in the value of the individual, his closeness to God, and his belief in God as the righteous judge allow him to voice his dilemma.

God does not give Jeremiah a direct answer as to why the wicked prosper. Instead, God's answer implies that since the wicked do prosper, Jeremiah must live with it and also look beyond it. The present difficulty is but a preparation for a more demanding future.

The *thicket of the Jordan* (verse 5) is the area in the Jordan Valley that is the home of wild animals.

God Laments Judah's Fate (12:7-13)

Several figures are used here for Judah, both the land and the people. These figures are *my house, my heritage* (NRSV; NIV = *inheritance*), *beloved, lion, speckled bird,* and *vineyard.*

In verse 13, the word *they* refers to Israel.

The *birds of prey* and *shepherds* are the destroyers.

This lament may come from 601 B.C. after Judah was attacked by several of her neighbors. Jehoiakim tried to revolt against Babylon, and Nebuchadnezzar sent some of his subject armies (the Chaldeans, Arameans, Moabites, and Ammonites) against Judah.

God Offers Hope for Other Nations (12:14-17)

When Judah returns from exile, her enemies will have the chance to live under the covenant.

The Sign of the Linen Waistcloth (13:1-11)

God orders Jeremiah to act out a sign (verses 1-7) and God interprets the sign (verses 8-11).

A waistcloth is an undergarment. (See the glossary.) The word translated *Euphrates* (NRSV) may instead mean *Parath* (so NIV). The Euphrates River is 400 miles from Judah, which would mean that Jeremiah completes his sign act only in a vision if "Euphrates" is the correct translation. Parath, however, may be at Parah which is five and one-half miles northeast of Jerusalem. At Parah there is a big spring that provided water for Jerusalem. Jeremiah could have traveled to Parah to complete his sign act so Parath may be the correct translation.

Other prophets also carry out sign acts (see, for example, Ezekiel 4:1-17; Isaiah 20:1-6) as part of their message. These acts catch people's attention and give the prophet an opportunity to interpret their meaning. These sign acts also carry the same dynamic power as prophetic speech. The acts set into motion the same creative force of God's will. They explain God's intentions for Israel and they are a visible demonstration of the consequences of God's intentions.

A Proverb Is Reinterpreted (13:12-14)

Jeremiah may have spoken this proverb and its new interpretation at a feast where much wine was consumed. The containers are *all the inhabitants of this land*, from the lowest to the highest. They will stagger from drinking the cup of God's wrath, which is the coming judgment (compare Jeremiah 25:15-16).

A Plea for Repentance (13:15-17)

Jeremiah again speaks against the people's false pride. This eloquent plea for repentance shows the depth of feeling Jeremiah has for the people and his sorrow at their fate. He may have issued this plea close to the time of the deportation of Israelites to Babylon in 598 B.C.

Oracle Against Jerusalem's Shame (13:18-27)

Verses 18-19 tell of Judah's fate after the Babylonian victory in 598/597 B.C. The king (verse 18) is Jehoiachin, who assumed the throne at the age of eighteen after Jehoiakim was killed. Jehoiachin reigned for three months before surrendering the city. His mother is Nehushta (see also 2 Kings 24:6-17).

The *Negeb* refers to the area in southern Judah, where the towns are closed against the Babylonian invaders. By this time, most of the territory of Judah had been taken over by foreigners.

Verses 20-27 are an oracle about the shame of Jerusalem. The woman/Jerusalem will be raped by the foe from the north, the Babylonians.

Jerusalem has lost her land and her people (*flock*) and will be under the rule of foreigners and foreign gods (former *allies*).

Verse 23 is a well-known and often-quoted wisdom saying. This proverb affirms the force of custom, habit, or training in human life. How can you do good if you are practiced or learned in doing evil?

Lament and Prayer Because of Drought (14:1-12)

Jeremiah describes the plight of the people and the beasts because of severe drought (verses 2-6). Rainfall is not only seasonal (see Jeremiah 5:24) but its concentration also varies. Much of the rain is concentrated in a limited number of days with dry periods in between. Areas for crops and pastures shift somewhat from year to year according to rainfall patterns.

The people prostate themselves on the ground (verse 2) and offer a prayer of remembrance (verses 7-9). In their need they remember God and call on God to remember them.

God rejects their prayers and their ritual (verses 10-12) because they do not remember God in their prosperous times.

Oracle Against False Prophets (14:13-16)

Jeremiah again denounces false prophecy. God expects the people of Israel to know false prophecy from the word of God. They will suffer for believing lies and false assurances of peace. These prophets are even prophesying in the Temple (*this place,* verse 13). They are perhaps also practicing the pagan arts of divination (obtaining supposedly secret knowledge other than words from God) in order to try to tell the future (see also Deuteronomy 18:10-11).

Lament, Prayer, God's Response (14:17-15:9)

This lament (verses 17-18) may come from a time during the siege of Jerusalem in 598 B.C. Those people outside the city are killed in battle; those inside the city are starving to death. As in the previous oracle, the priests and prophets with no knowledge of God, no commitment to God's word, leave the people helpless. The true word of God is as necessary for life as are food and water.

Verses 19-22 are a prayer of repentance in which the people plead their case before God. Apparently this plea is made during a drought (see verse 22). The false prophets tell of peace, but none is to be found. The people can only throw themselves on God's mercy. They hope that God will not allow the divine name to be dishonored among other nations by allowing the people called by God's name to die.

Your glorious throne is Zion, or specifically, the Holy of Holies in the Temple.

God responds in 15:1-4 and 5:9. The pleas for mercy are too late. Even Moses and Samuel, two of the greatest men in all Israel, could not intercede at this point.

Sheep dogs were rarely, if ever, used in Palestine. Dogs were considered about like jackals (verse 3). Instead, the shepherd established a close relationship with his flock. The sheep recognized his voice and would stay with him.

Manasseh (verse 4) introduced pagan cults into Judah (see also 2 Kings 21).

Verses 15:5-9 may come from a time after the siege and deportation of 598 B.C.

Winnowing of grain is done by tossing the threshed grain into the air so the wind will blow away the chaff and the heavier kernels will fall to the ground. A winnowing fork is a wooden pitchfork with long, broad prongs.

Jeremiah's Second Personal Lament (15:10-21)

Jeremiah again confronts God with the burden he bears because God's hand is upon him. God promises Jeremiah support through his trials (verses 19-21). Verses 13-14 apparently belong in chapter 17 (see 17:3-4).

Jeremiah's lament probably comes from a period in which he met repeated opposition and oppression, perhaps toward the end of Jehoiakim's reign.

God knew Jeremiah and marked him for prophecy before his birth (Jeremiah 1:5). Jeremiah now deeply regrets this. He expresses his despair by using the word *alas* (NIV; NRSV = *woe*), which is a word used in mourning. Instead of bringing a life-giving word, he brings conflict and contention. He is persecuted, ostracized, and must forego the normal human expressions of merriment and joy.

When Jeremiah ate God's words (see also Ezekiel 3:1-3), he became a vessel of God's words and he incorporated these words into himself. Yet God's hand, instead of being an inspiration, now is oppressive and brings gloom.

A *deceitful* or *deceptive brook* (verse 18) may be a stream that cannot be relied upon because it has water only after a heavy rainfall. This is yet another of the many illustrations and images from nature that Jeremiah uses.

Jeremiah must return to God, repent of his self-pity and despair, and deliver his message if the people are to turn to God. The opposition to Jeremiah's message will continue, but God will strengthen and protect him.

§ § § § § § §

The Message of Jeremiah 11-15

Despite the years of Jeremiah's prophetic warnings, Judah continues to live in false pride, sin, and shame. What do the oracles of chapters 11–15 tell us about the relationship among God, Jeremiah, and Judah at this time?

§ God mourns for "the beloved of my soul" but will not turn aside the "sword of the Lord" which must punish Judah.

§ Jeremiah grows weary, angry, and fearful in his duties to Israel.

§ The people sometimes turn to God in times of acute distress. Most of the time, however, they follow their covenant responsibilities while counting on God to uphold them.

§ § § § § § §

Jeremiah 16–19

Introduction to These Chapters

These chapters tell of physical symbols of Judah's fate (Jeremiah 18:1-12; 19:1-15) and of a personal symbol (Jeremiah 16:1-13). Jeremiah is again driven to voice his complaints to God because of the continuing opposition to his message and the plots against his life (Jeremiah 17:14-18; 18:18-23). Here is an outline of these chapters:

I. Jeremiah's Life Is to Be a Symbol (16:1-21)
    A. Jeremiah is not to have a family (16:1-13)
    B. Oracle of eventual deliverance (16:14-15)
    C. There will be no refuge for Israel (16:16-18)
    D. All nations will turn to God (16:19-21)
II. Oracles Against Backsliders (17:1-13)
III. Jeremiah Prays for Vindication (17:14-18)
IV. Teachings About the Sabbath (17:19-27)
V. A Sign and a Lament (17:1-23)
    A. The sign of the potter's vessel (17:1-12)
    B. Oracle against Israel's stubbornness (18:13-17)
    C. Jeremiah laments opposition (18:18-23)
VI. A Sign of Judah's Fate (19:1-15)

Jeremiah Is Not to Have a Family (16:1-13)

Jeremiah's life is to be a sign for others as to what God has in store for Israel. He is denied the comfort and blessing of a family of his own. He will have no children to carry on his name. He is denied the communion with others that comes from sharing times of sorrow and joy.

This part of Jeremiah's life is to be a sign that the

familiar rites of consolation and celebration no longer have a place in Israel's life. The people are to ask why, and Jeremiah must explain that the people broke the covenant and were stubborn and full of pride. Israel will instead serve foreigners (*serve other gods*).

For a body to be left unburied so that dogs, jackals, and vultures eat the flesh is a dreaded disgrace (verse 4). A corpse is considered unclean, and an unburied corpse causes the land to be unclean. In the Old Testament, anything is unclean that is offensive to the holiness of God. This can be a physical, ritual, or moral uncleanness.

Details of normal mourning ritual are given in verses 5-7. Mourners usually fast until the evening of the day of burial. Since the corpse makes the home unclean, neighbors bring in food and wine at the end of the day and during the period of mourning. (See Jeremiah 9:17-22 for more details of mourning ritual.)

Oracle of Eventual Deliverance (16:14-15)

These verses duplicate most of Jeremiah 23:7-8 and are probably from a later time than 16:1-13. Israel's eventual return from exile is seen as a new Exodus.

There Will Be No Refuge for Israel (16:16-18)

These verses continue the thought of verses 1-13. They explain that nothing escapes God's knowledge and no one will escape the Babylonians.

All Nations Will Turn to God (16:19-21)

These verses follow the line of thought from verses 14-15. Israel's return from exile wil be part of a larger fulfillment in which all nations will know and follow God's word.

Oracles Against Backsliders (17:1-13)

Judah is hardened in sin. The evidence is both interal (*their heart*) and external (*their altars*).

Verse 1 describes an iron stylus with a diamond tip

that can cut into hard surfaces such as rock or gem stones. Jeremiah sees that sin is engraved on Israel's stubborn, or hard, heart (see also Jeremiah 16:12). In the future, however, God's law will be engraved on her heart (see also Jeremiah 31:33).

The *horns* of the altar (verse 1) are projections at each of the corners of the altar (see also Exodus 27:2). In some sacrifices, blood is smeared on these horns (Leviticus 4:7). In the context of this oracle, the horns symbolize Israel's empty sacrifices. The people make sacrifices to God but also to idols. *Asherah* (NIV) can mean both the proper name of a goddess and the pillars or trees that are the objects of worship in her cult (so NRSV).

Verses 5-8 are a psalm on which Psalm 1 is probably based. This hymn explains that our choice of where we place our trust, either in God or in humankind, leads to either blessings or curses in our lives. The arm of flesh is no real source of strength.

Verses 9-10 are a wisdom saying that seems not to agree with the previous discussion between Jeremiah and God about the fate of the wicked and the righteous (Jeremiah 12:1-6). Jeremiah poses the question in verse 9 and God answers in verse 10. The proverb of verse 11 elaborates on this and explains that the wicked eventually will pay.

The exact meaning of verses 12-13 is uncertain. They appear to contrast the eternal and living nature of God and God's sanctuary (perhaps the Temple) with those who turn away from God and are like dust. Given Jeremiah's attitude that the physical presence of the Temple is no guarantee of God's favor, the throne may be symbolic rather than meaning the actual Temple.

Jeremiah Prays for Vindication (17:14-18)

This lament comes from a time when Judah is not under a direct threat from Babylon. Perhaps the time is around 601 B.C. when the Babylonians are engaged against the Eygptians and temporarily withdraw from Jerusalem.

Jeremiah's opponents taunt him because his words of disaster have not been fulfilled. He still does not desire God's judgment, but he has grown weary of the abuse he suffers because of his message. At this moment, he is willing for judgment to come so that he may be vindicated and his persecutors silenced.

Teachings About the Sabbath (17:19-27)

This oracle may be put here to complement the oracle in verses 1-4 which mentions violations in worship (verse 2).

In other passages, Jeremiah denounces the form of ritual and law that is without substance (for example, Jeremiah 6:20; 7:8-10). This passage emphasizes the strict observance of sabbath laws as the basis for the continued existence of Judah. Strict observance of the sabbath did serve a purpose, however. The Israelites were in exile in Babylon and were under foreign domination in Judah. During this time, strict observance of the sabbath set the Israelites apart from the dominant pagan culture and worship practices.

The Sign of the Potter's Vessel (18:1-12)

The shaping of a vessel in the potter's hands illustrates the power of God to shape human destiny. This image is similar to that of God shaping Adam in the Garden of Eden (Genesis 2:7). In contrast to the clay of the potter, which has no will of its own, Israel does have a choice in how she is shaped. If Israel chooses evil, God, the master potter, will shape evil against her.

The workshop Jeremiah visited probably consisted of a room where the potter sat at his wheel forming vessels and where pots awaiting finishing were stored. The wheel may have been made of a pair of stones, one on top of the other. A cone-shaped protrusion on the bottom stone fit into a socket on the top one. A small room for storing pots ready for firing would have been next to the kiln. The area around the kiln and workshop probably contained a well or basin for water, piles of new clay being weathered, and piles of sherds (scrap pottery), ashes, and slag.

Potters played a major role in Irsaelite society. Their importance is reflected in the many Old Testament references to the potters' craft and vessels.

Oracle Against Israel's Stubbornness (18:13-17)

This poem gives examples of the stubbornness and rebelliousness referred to in verse 12. A nation forsaking her own god is unnatural and unheard of even among pagans.

Verse 14 envisions Mount Hermon in Phoenicia, which is 9,100 feet above sea level. Its top is usually covered with snow the year round.

The *mountain waters* (NRSV; NIV = *cool waters*) are streams that do not depend on rainwater for their flow.

The *ancient roads* are the ways of the covenant.

A hiss is a sign of astonishment or of contempt. People may hiss when passing ruins as protection against demons of destruction (see also Jeremiah 19:8). Hissing is often accompanied by wagging the head (verse 16), clapping the hands, gnashing the teeth (see Lamentations 2:15-16), and by shaking the fist (see Zephaniah 2:15).

The *east wind* is a shamsin or sirocco. It is a hot, dry, dusty wind coming off the deserts to the south and southeast of Judah. This wind often blows for several days at a time during the spring and fall. It brings high temperature, low humidity, and much dust.

Jeremiah Laments Opposition (18:18-23)

This lament is in response to continued persecution of Jeremiah. It may come from a time late in the reign of King Jehoiakim when opposition to Jeremiah is strong.

Verse 18 speaks of three different groups of religious leaders and the special prerogative claimed by each group:

(1) The priests consider themselves the guardians and interpreters of the law in questions about worship, temple practices, and other religious matters.

(2) The *wise* are official advisors in the kings' court (see also Jeremiah 8:8-9) whose function is to provide counsel, both political and spiritual, to the king.

(3) The prophets may also be officials of the court who are to mediate the word of God to the king.

Jeremiah is bitter because he had prayed to God for mercy on their behalf (for example, Jeremiah 15:11), but he receives only evil in return. Instead of mercy, he now prays for merciless destruction on them.

A Sign of Judah's Fate (19:1-15)

These verses may be divided into the following sections:

(1) God tells Jeremiah what to buy and where to go (verses 1-2)

(2) God tells Jeremiah to list Judah's crimes (verses 3-5) and to declare punishment (verses 6-9)

(3) A sign is enacted (verse 10)

(4) The sign is interpreted (verses 11-13)

(5) Punishment is declared in the Temple (verses 14-15)

A flask is a water decanter with a narrow neck. Its name in Hebrew comes from the gurgling sound made as water is poured out of it. Such pitchers are artiscially made and are expensive to buy.

Jeremiah probably visited a potter who lived just outside the walls of Jerusalem in the Hinnom Valley. The Potsherd Gate (19:2) in the southern wall of the old city probably gets its name from the nearby piles of broken and scrap pottery *(sherds)* around the potters' workshops.

Pagan worship and human sacrifice are again named as Judah's crimes.

Therefore days are coming announced the punishment. Days brings to mind the day of the Lord, which will not be a day of victory for Israel but rather a day of defeat. Evidence of this reversal will be seen in the change of the name *Topeth to Slaughter.* At the place where Judah once slaughtered her innocent children to pagan gods, the people of Judah will fall to the swords of the enemy. They will be denied the dignity of a decent burial. Beautiful Jerusalem will be an object of horror.

There is a play on words in Hebrew between the words for *jar* or *jug* (verses 1 and 10) and *make void* or *ruin* (verse 10). The idol-worshiping city, like the flask, will be broken and wasted.

Famine during the siege will cause the people to resort to cannibalism.

The flat roofs of houses are used for pagan worship ceremonies (verse 13). The *host* of heaven are pagan deities. Incense is burned in religious ceremonies so that its pleasing odors will please the gods. Incense is used in the Temple both as a pleasing odor to God and to help cover up the odor of burning flesh from the animal sacrifices.

Drink offerings (NIV; NRSV = *libations*) means wine.

§ § § § § § §

The Message of Jeremiah 16-19

The prophet's life is taken over by the Word he must declare. Jeremiah is called to act as well as to speak. What do prophetic sign acts accomplish?

§ Sign acts get people's attention.

§ These acts give the prophet an opportunity to explain the action and to explain how God's Word applies to it.

§ The sign acts give people visual as well as verbal food for thought. They encourage people to look for God's truth even when it comes in surprising ways.

§ Sign acts set in motion the accomplishment of God's Word because they have creative power just like the prophetic word.

§ § § § § § §

Jeremiah 20–22

Introduction to These Chapters

Jeremiah 20:1-6 describes the consequences of
Jeremiah's word and actions in chapter 19. The
remainder of chapter 20 contains two more of Jeremiah's
personal laments. This concludes the group of oracles
that come, in general, from the time of King Jehoiakim.
Chapters 21–25 are oracles from the reign of King
Zedekiah (597–587 B.C.).

Here is an outline of chapters 20–22:
  I. Jeremiah's Suffering and Lamentation (20:1-18)
     A. Jeremiah is beaten and confined (20:1-6)
     B. Jeremiah accuses God (20:7-13)
     C. Jeremiah laments his birth (20:14-18)
 II. Oracle Against Zedekiah and Jerusalem (21:1-10)
III. Oracles About the Royal House (21:11-22:30)
     A. Oracle to the king of Judah (21:11-14)
     B. Oracle to the king (22:1-9)
     C. Oracle concerning King Shallum (22:10-12)
     D. Oracle concerning King Jehoiakim (22:13-19)
     E. Oracle concerning Jerusalem (22:20-23)
     F. Oracle concerning King Jehoiachin (22:24-30)

Jeremiah's Suffering and Lamentation (20:1-18)

Jeremiah's sermon in the Temple angers a temple
official so that he beats Jeremiah and confines Jeremiah
to stocks in the Temple (verses 1-6). This report is

followed by two laments (verses 7-13, 14-18). Jeremiah lists his complaints against God and curses the day he was born.

Chapter 20 closes the collection of oracles from Jehoiakim's reign and is representative of what Jeremiah faced in his prophecy during those years. He suffered physical and mental abuse at the hands of his enemies. He was spiritually and emotionally distraught. At this point, he had been in his ministry some twenty-seven to twenty-eight years. These years had been hard, and he was no longer a young man. There were no signs that the people of Israel were turning back to God. There were many signs, however, that Judah's life as a nation was nearing its end.

Jeremiah Is Beaten and Confined (20:1-6)

Pashhur is probably the head of the Temple police. His duty is to see that order is kept in the Temple and that no unauthorized people come in. He is probably among those deported to Babylon in 598 B.C. as Jeremiah prophesies, because someone else is chief officer after that time (see Jeremiah 29:25-26).

The upper Benjamin Gate is probably on the north side of the Temple. It is a gate into the Temple area itself, not a gate into the city.

Stocks are wooden frames in which a prisoner's hands and feet are locked. Jeremiah spends one night in confinement.

Jeremiah Accuses God (20:7-13)

Jeremiah first describes the hold God has on him and its effects (verses 7-10). He follows this description with a hymn of praise for God's deliverance (verses 11-13).

These verses reveal the strength of Jeremiah's sense of being called, even compelled, to prophesy. The persecutions Jeremiah endures and his inner struggles do not sway his conviction that he has a divine commission.

He has a strong sense of God's direction. Yet, he does not seem to lose a sense of himself, either. Jeremiah is not in a frenzy of ecstacy, nor is he removed from human reality. He carries a burden for his people. He is the vessel and spokesman for God's word, but he is still a man who suffers. Indeed, Jeremiah suffers *because* he bears God's word, not in spite of it.

The verb *deceived* (NIV; NRSV = *enticed*) is a strong one in Hebrew. This form is used elsewhere in the Old Testament to mean *to seduce* and to describe a lying spirit. The strength of this word reveals the depth of feeling in Jeremiah's accusation. He does not say this to God lightly.

In spite of the feeling that he has been deceived, Jeremiah cannot hold back his message. God is in control. (See also Amos 3:8; 1 Corinthians 9:16.)

Even Jeremiah's friends denounce him. The prophet faces *terror on every side* (verse 10), just as his enemies will one day (verse 3). However, Jeremiah still must praise God (verses 11-13). God will answer his needs. Jeremiah uses the hymns of worship to express his confidence in and praise of God. (See also Psalm 6:9-10; 31:3; 109:30; 140:12-13.)

Jeremiah Laments His Birth (20:14-18)

In this lament Jeremiah curses his own existence (see also Jeremiah 15:10).

A day of birth, particularly the birth of a son, was a blessed day in Israelite life. Children were valued as a blessing from the Lord, and to be childless was a great tragedy. If the father was not present for the birth, someone would be sent to tell him whether the child and mother were healthy and whether the child was a boy or girl.

Jeremiah curses the messenger who bore the news of his birth. Had Jeremiah died at birth, he would have passed into darkness and rest, avoiding the trials of life.

Verse 16 refers to Sodom and Gomorrah (see Genesis 19).

This lament must come from a particularly hard time in Jeremiah's life, perhaps after his arrest and imprisonment. With even his friends turning on him and no reprieve in sight for Israel, Jeremiah is exhausted and despondent.

Oracle Against Zedekiah and Jerusalem (21:1-10)

Chapter 21 begins the collection of material from the reign of King Zedekiah.

Historical Background

In 601 B.C., Egypt again tried to exert its power against Babylon in the continuing battle to divide what had been Assyria and assert control over Palestine, which had valuable trade and military routes. Egypt defeated Babylonian forces in battle that year, but it was not a decisive victory. Babylon fell back only temporarily. Nevertheless, King Jehoiakim decided to try to throw off Babylonian control altogether. He withheld the tribute or taxes demanded by Babylon. Nebuchadnezzar retaliated at first by having some of his vassal armies raid Judah.

By 598 B.C. Nebuchadnezzar was ready to move against Judah in force. Jehoiakim was killed during this time, either assassinated by some of his own men or in a military skirmish.

In December of 598 B.C., Babylonian forces laid siege to Jerusalem, Jehoiachin, who had assumed the throne after his father's death, surrendered the city within three months.

The royal family, court officials, artisans, soldiers, and leading citizens were deported to Babylon. According to 2 Kings 24:14, ten thousand people were taken into exile. Jeremiah 52:28 says that 3,023 Jews were deported, but this figure may include only adult males. Temple treasures were also taken to Babylon. Jerusalem itself was not destroyed. Nebuchadnezzar put Zedekiah, Jehoiachin's uncle and Jehoiakim's brother, on the throne of Judah.

Jeremiah 21:1-20 is out of chronological sequence. The events it describes are probably from the Babylonian siege of 587 B.C. at the end of Zedekiah's reign.

Zedekaih often asks Jeremiah both publicly and secretly to inquire of the Lord for him. Zedekiah seeks an oracle, a prophetic message, concerning God's will. He apparently believes that Jeremiah is a true prophet. But he is weak and does not commit himself to follow Jeremiah's word against the pressures of those who oppose Jeremiah.

Jeremiah says Judah must surrender to the Babylonians and accept their rule as just punishment from God. Only by submitting to God's will can Judah find her way back to God. Surrender is defeat in human terms. But in God's plan, surrender leads to life. This statement echoes the commands of Deuteronomy 30:15-16 to choose life in the covenant instead of death apart from God.

To *set one's face against* (verse 10, NRSV; NIV = *I have determined*) is an expression of hostility. The face indicates God is present, but this presence is for harm and *not for good*. Jerusalem was not completely destroyed in the siege of 598 B.C. The Temple was burned and the city walls broken down in the siege of 587 B.C.

Oracles About the Royal House (21:11-22:30)

This is a series of oracles about the royal family of Judah. Some are general and others are directed to a specific king. Prophets traditionally hold the right to criticize a king. They stand on God's behalf before both king and people. As the chief judicial officer in Israel, the king is not subject to humanly executed prosecution. Neither are penalities imposed on priests, prophets, and government officials for most moral and ethical violations of their duties. Punishment for their crimes is announced by the prophet.

Oracle to the King of Judah (21:11-14)

This oracle could be applied to any of Judah's kings. However, it is particularly appropriate for Jehoiakim, whom Jeremiah elsewhere condemns for injustice (see Jeremiah 22:17).

The king's duties include settling legal disputes. Israel's citizens are entitled to fair treatment before the law. The king must answer to God for not carrying out his proper responsibilities.

Verse 13 may refer to Jerusalem and to the royal palace (see also 1 Kings 7:23).

Oracle to the King (22:1-9)

This oracle expands on Jeremiah 21:11-14.

Go *down* may mean that Jeremiah is in the Temple area from which he will go to the palace. The palace adjoins the Temple but is on a lower level.

If this oracle is directed at Jehoiakim, verse 3 may refer to his oppression of the people of Judah in order to raise money both to pay the tribute demanded by Egypt and to build himself new palaces.

Gilead is noted for its balm, its flocks of goats, and its trees. The *summit* of *Lebanon* is the highest part of Lebanon which is famous for its forests.

Cedar may be a reference to the cedarwood palace of the king.

The ruins of Jerusalem will be a witness and a wonder even to non-Israelites in the years to come (verses 8-9).

Oracle Concerning King Shallum (22:10-12)

Shallum is the personal name of Jehoahaz who was king of Judah for a brief time in 609 B.C. When Josiah was killed, Jehoahaz became king. After three months, the

Egyptians took him to Egypt (*from this place,* verse 11) and made Jehoiakim king.

Him who is dead is Josiah. *Him who goes away* (NRSV; NIV = *exiled*) is Jehoahaz (verse 10).

Oracle Concerning King Jehoiakim (22:13-19)

Jeremiah's strongest condemnations in this series of oracles are against Jehoiakim. Second Kings 23:24-24:7 gives details of the reign of Josiah, the transition of power to Jehoiakim, and the reign of Jehoiakim. The account in 2 Kings supports the charges of injustice and oppression that Jeremiah makes against Jehoiakim. The historical narrative does not give any details of his death. Second Kings 24:6 says that *Jehoiakim slept with his fathers,* a phrase which usually means that a person was buried in a family tomb.

His neighbor (verse 13 NRSV; NIV = *countrymen*) refers to the king's subjects who were forced to work for him for no wages. The kings of Judah were not supposed to be despots but were to be righteous *shepherds* of the people. With the creation of the monarchy and the centralization of authority it imposed, the Israelites gave up some individual freedom. They had to pay taxes to the government, serve in the military, and, at times, labor without pay in service to the king. A governmental bureaucracy developed that was open to corruption and self-preservation.

Jeremiah compares Jehoiakim to his father, Josaih (verses 15-17).

Verse 15 refers to Jehoiakim's luxurious palace, which he perhaps believed set him apart as king or made him more grand than other kings.

In contrast, Josiah was content with the simple necessities of life, to *eat and drink* (verse 15). He upheld his duties in dispensing justice to those in need. Thus, he had true knowledge of God—knowledge that is not just intellectual but also is evident in moral actions.

Oracle Concerning Jerusalem (22:20-23)

Here Jerusalem (Israel) is personified as a woman. *Your lovers* (NRSV; NIV = *allies*) are the leaders of Jerusalem or are the false gods the people have worshiped. *Your shepherds* are the leaders of the people. Verse 23 may refer to the king in his cedar palace or to Judah in general. (See also Jeremiah 22:6-7, 14-15.)

Oracle Concerning King Jehoiachin (22:24-30)

Coniah is the personal name of Jehoiachin (also called Jeconiah in Jeremiah 24:1). Even after his deportation to Babylon, many Israelites, both in Judah and in exile, still considered him the legitimate king. They expected Jehoiakim to be allowed to return to Jerusalem soon (see Jeremiah 28:1-4). Jeremiah apparently does not consider him the legitimate king and instead supports Zedekiah.

A signet ring is a valuable personal possession. According to 1 Chronicles 3:17, Jehoiachin had seven sons. Cunieform tablets from Babylon record that rations of oil were provided for Jehoiachin and his five sons during their captivity. Though one of his grandsons was governor of Judah for a time, none of Jehoiachin's descendants ever ruled as king in Judah. In this sense, Jehoiachin was childless.

§ § § § § § §

The Message of Jeremiah 20–22

These chapters deal with issues of authority: Who is really in charge in Israel? These oracles and laments answer that God is in charge.

§ Jeremiah may complain bitterly to God about his duties and the consequences of these duties. Nevertheless, God knew Jeremiah and appointed him a prophet even before his birth. Jeremiah is bound to speak God's Word.

§ The kings of Judah are not the ultimate authority over God's people. Their office is a trust and a responsibility from God to whom they must answer for their actions.

§ Even pagan kings serve God's purposes. King Nebuchadrezzar of Babylon is God's instrument of punishment against Judah.

§ No one, high or low, is outside of God's authority. In particular, people to whom much power is entrusted are held strictly accountable for the use of that power.

§ § § § § § §

Jeremiah 23–25

Introduction to These Chapters

After the sweeping condemnations of Zedekiah, Jehoiakim, and Jehoiachin, Jeremiah offers an oracle of hope concerning future leaders. The rest of the material in this section (23:9–25:38 contains oracles and a vision report that announce judgment on other groups of leaders—false prophets, the remnant in Jerusalem, the people of Israel, and other nations. Here is an outline of these chapters:

    I. A Hopeful Oracle About Future Leaders (23:1-8)
   II. Oracles Concerning the Prophets (23:9-40)
      A. Both prophet and priest are wicked (23:9-12)
      B. Evil deeds of Jerusalem's prophets (23:13-15)
      C. False prophets denounced (23:16-22)
      D. The false prophets' lying dreams (23:23-32)
      E. The burden of the Lord (23:33-40)
  III. The Vision of the Basket of Figs (24:1-10)
  IV. Oracle About the Seventy-year Exile (25:1-14)
   V. Oracle Concerning the Nations (25:15-38)

A Hopeful Oracle About Future Leaders (23:1-8)

This oracle delivers both a condemnation of evil shepherds and a promise of righteous leaders to come. Leaders of the people of Israel are condemned for not performing their proper duties (verses 1-4). The figure of the shepherd is often used in the Old Testament both for the king and for ruling officials in general (see also

Ezekiel 34). If this oracle is from the time of Zedekiah, then the evil shepherds are probably officials and counselors in the government.

Jeremiah does not condemn Zedekiah personally in the same way he does the previous kings. Rather, the prophet finds Zedekiah to be weak and prone to listen to the false counsel of his advisors instead of to the true word of God. These advisors plot rebellion against Babylon instead of submitting to their punishment as God's will.

Verses 5-8 promise that a king from David's line will one day rule over a restored Israel. The return from exile will be a new Exodus (verses 7-8). This *righteous branch* will attend properly to the *flock* Israel. In Hebrew, the name *The Lord is our righteousness* is a play on the name Zedekiah, which means God *is my righteousness*. The word *righteousness* means *in right relationship* to God and also means salvation or deliverance. Jeremiah's play on words points out that Zedekiah is king in name only. In contrast, the future ruler will be king in substance and in name.

In this oracle, people and events from Israel's past are used to help explain the future. The people are asked to remember their past relationship with God and to let this relationship be a guide in their present problems.

Oracles Concerning the Prophets (23:9-40)

This collection of oracles comes after the oracles against the kings and rulers. Prophets, rulers, and priests are in positions of power in Israelite life.

Jeremiah refers to false prophets more than any other prophet in the Old Testament. Many prophets and priests from local sanctuaries probably came to Jerusalem after Josiah closed these sanctuaries and centralized worship at the Jerusalem Temple. Jeremiah had to contend with them, especially with those whom he believed gave false prophecy and did not appreciate the gravity of their office.

Both Prophet and Priest Are Wicked (23:9-12)

Because Jeremiah knows the true word of God concerning Israel, the false words and evil deeds of the prophets and priests bring Jeremiah great distress. The prophets and priests are supposed to be the guardians of Israel's faith but they practice their wickedness even in the Temple. Elsewhere in the Old Testament, priests are accused of failing to follow divine instruction and of being eager to receive inappropriate compensation for their services. Some priests may have even offered sacrifices in the Temple both to God and to pagan deities.

Some prophets are accused of failing to receive a true word from God because of their moral or spiritual failings. They declare their own imaginings, prophesy in the name of pagan gods, and shape their words to suit those who reward them financially or to please the king.

The *pastures* of the wilderness (verse 10) are those in the arid regions of Palestine which are dependent on seasonal rains to produce grass (see Jeremiah 2:2, 6). The curse is of God (see also Jeremiah 17:5-6).

Their sin carries with it their own undoing (*their path will become slippery,* verse 12). They reap what they sow.

Evil Deeds of Jerusalem's Prophets (23:13-15)

Samaria is the capital of the Northern Kingdom, which was taken over by Assyria in 722 B.C.

Baal is a Canaanite fertility god. The Israelites had dealings with this cult beginning with their entrance into Canaan (approximately 1200 B.C.). They went through alternate periods of repressing the cult and adapting it into their worship practices.

The Jerusalem prophets may commit literal adultery and/or figurative adultery by abandoning the covenant and turning to idols. Sexual intercourse was part of the ritual of some fertility cults.

They *strengthen the hands of evil doers* by declaring a false peace to the people of Jerusalem (see Jeremiah 6:14-15) and by allowing money to influence their prophecy (Jeremiah 23:16-17).

False Prophets Denounced (23:16-22)

This oracle denounces the messages of these false prophets and is addressed to the people of Jerusalem. The people are hearing many voices claiming to have the true word of God. The people must discern for themselves who speaks the truth (see Jeremiah 14:13-14).

Vain hopes are the prophets' promises of an early end to Babylonian rule and of the return of Jehoiachin to Judah.

The basis of Jeremiah's renunciation is that none of these prophets is truly called by God.

In heaven, the council of the Lord (verse 18) is the assembly of God and the hosts of heaven. God's council is also the word given to one who is called by God and stands in God's presence.

The latter days (verse 20) are the coming days of judgment.

The False Prophets' Lying Dreams (23:23-32)

In the Old Testament, dreamers are associated with diviners, soothsayers, sorcerers, enchanters, and magicians (see also Jeremiah 27:8-9). Most practices of these occult arts are forbidden in Israelite law (see Deuteronomy 18:10-12).

Joseph (Genesis 40:12; 41:15) and Daniel (Daniel 2) are honored as interpreters of dreams. Their skill, however, came from God. Dream interpretation in association with idolatry is condemned. Jeremiah condemns the dreams that are from the prophets' own minds and not from God. The prophets declare false words, perhaps in order to relieve the people's, or their own, anxiety about the future. Instead of listening to God, they listen to their own lies. Jeremiah again declares that knowledge of and from God is the only true knowledge.

The Burden (NRSV) or Oracle (NIV) of the Lord (23:33-40)

The word *burden* is used in two senses in this passage. When the people ask, "What is the *burden* of the Lord?" it means an *oracle* or message from God. This meaning may come from the belief that the message of a prophet is a burden placed by God on the prophet: The prophet then is to place the burden on the nation or individual receiving the message. In this sense, burden is used most often of a message of punishment or disaster. Here Jeremiah testifies that he sometimes felt his prophetic message to be a personal burden (see for example, Jeremiah 20:7-14).

Then the prophet replies, "You are the *burden*" (verse 33). This means a literal burden, from a Hebrew root word which means *to lift up.*

This word play is another example of Jeremiah's creative use of language to get his prophecy across to the people.

Verses 34-40 expand on Jeremiah's oracle in verse 33. The exact meaning, both in Hebrew and in English, is not entirely clear. The verses perhaps mean that people should seek a true answer from the prophet, not a burden or message which is, in reality, just *the burden of every man's own word.*

The Vision of the Baskets of Figs (24:1-10)

Smiths are Israelite metalworkers (verse 1).

Figs are typically eaten at the end of a meal. Since the people had no refined sugar, figs were prized for their sweetness.

In general, a vision is a communication from God of

something which is available only through God's power and initiative. To true prophets, a vision is a revelation of God's word. The vision discloses something of God and of God's purposes in relation to God's people. Jeremiah's vision of the two baskets of figs comes after 598 B.C.

Ezekiel 11:14-21 also speaks of those who are left in Jerusalem in contrast to those in exile. Apparently, some of the people left in Jerusalem felt that the exiles were suffering as sinners under God's judgment, while they enjoyed God's grace in their possession of the homeland. The people in Jerusalem have not given up their idolatry, however.

The people in Jerusalem are condemned, according to Jeremiah, to be exiles themselves. Those in exile will be brought back to Judah to live in a renewed relationship to God. Their hearts will no longer be stubborn and prideful.

In biblical usage, the heart is very important in personal life. The heart is the place where all the forces of human life come together. These forces include emotion, intellect, will, and physical being. A person's character is shaped by the thoughts, plans, hopes, fears, attitudes, and actions of the heart.

Jeremiah's prophecy concerning the exiles in verses 4-9 does not mean that they were all good. Ezekiel prophesied against idolators both among the exiles (Ezekiel 14:1-11) and among those left in Jerusalem (Ezekiel 21:1-2). Nor, in fact, do all the exiles return to Judah after they are given the chance to do so in 539 B.C. According to Jeremiah and Ezekiel, it is with those who do return that the hope of Judah lies.

Those who live in Egypt are perhaps those Judeans who went to Egypt in 609 B.C. along with King Jehoahaz.

Oracle About the Seventy-Year Exile (25:1-14)

This oracle may at one time have been the conclusion to Jeremiah's memoirs which he dictated to Baruch in 605/604 B.C. (see Jeremiah 36:1-4).

The Babylonians defeated the Egyptians at Carchemish in June of 605 B.C. Nebuchadrezzar's father died later that summer and Nebuchadrezzar became king. Jeremiah says that Jehoiakim's fourth year as king is Nebuchadrezzar's first year as king of Babylon. According to Daniel 1:1, Jehoiakim's third year is Nebuchadrezzar's first.

The Babylonian method of record keeping does not count the months Nebuchadrezzar served as king between the coronation and the next year. The months between September 605 B.C. and April 604 B.C. are known as his ascension year. Daniel uses this method of counting the years. Jeremiah uses the Judean system which counts the ascension months as the first year.

Jeremiah reminds his listeners how long they have refused to hear God's word and obey. Nebuchadrezzar is called God's servant. He is God's agent of punishment for the people of Israel. The Babylonians and the Israelites are both under God's control.

The number seventy (verse 12) may be a round or symbolic number rather than a specific one. The number seven and its multiples are often used in the Old Testament as sacred numbers signifying completeness. The number seventy, however, is close to the number of years between this oracle by Jeremiah in 605 B.C. and the proclamation by Cyrus of Persia in 539 B.C. allowing the exiles to return to Judah (see Ezra 1:1-3).

Oracle Concerning the Nations (25:15-38)

This section may be divided into a vision report (verses 15-29) and an oracle of judgment (verses 16-38). These passages may have introduced the section of oracles against the nations (Jeremiah 46–51) at one stage in the collection of Jeremiah's words.

In this vision, Jeremiah sees a cup of wine which he takes from God and carries to all the nations God will punish. The *cup of the wine of wrath* symbolizes God's righteous anger and punishment. In verse 16 this cup is equated with the sword.

The nations, city-states, and tribes listed here are Judah's neighbors. (See the Glossary for identification of each.)

In verse 28 Jeremiah offers the cup with the same force that he offers the word. The word of God will be declared and its purposes fulfilled for everyone who lives upon the earth (verse 29).

The oracle in verses 30-38 describes the coming of God in judgment against all flesh (verse 31). Judgment is described in images used elsewhere in Jeremiah and in the works of other prophets—a great noise, treading of grapes, a courtroom, mourning rituals, and the sword.

The leaders of the people are to mourn their own deaths (verse 34).

§ § § § § § §

The Message of Jeremiah 23–25

Jeremiah offers two notes of hope in these oracles. First, Israel may look forward to a future day when a truly righteous king will rule over them (compare Isaiah 11; Zechariah 3:8). Second, the nation which punishes Israel will itself be punished after seventy years. His message is not entirely gloomy.

In the meantime, sin must be dealt with, especially the sins of the false prophets, priests, and other dishonest leaders. Oracles of judgment are declarations of God's punishment for sin. The basis for such declarations by Jeremiah and by other prophets is found in the nature of sin itself. What may we learn from this about sin?

§ In broad terms, the Bible sees sin as personal alienation from God. Sins of any kind are, first of all, sins against God.

§ The Old Testament understanding of ritual, moral, and spiritual sins rests on the recognition of God's own moral being.

§ Through what is sinful in relation to the will and being of God, we understand what is sinful in relation to one another. Because of this, our sins against our another affect our relationship to God.

§ According to the Old Testament prophets, the standard of moral good is God's revealed will. Sins against this standard are a violation of the covenant relationship that has been established between God and God's people.

§ § § § § § §

Jeremiah 26–28

Introduction to These Chapters

Jeremiah 26 begins a series of chapters (26–45) that
contain biographical information about Jeremiah. Much
of this material is drawn from Jeremiah's memoirs that
were written by his scribe, Baruch (see Jeremiah 36:1-4).
Chapters 26–29 tell of Jeremiah's conflict with Judean
religious leaders—the priests and especially the
prophets. Each chapter is dated according to the reign of
the king of Judah at the time, and each chapter comes
from a different time.

Here is an outline of chapters 26–28:
I. Jeremiah's Temple Sermon (26:1-24)
  A. Summary of the sermon (26:1-6)
  B. Report of Jeremiah's arrest and trial (26:7-24)
II. Oracles Concerning the King of Babylon (27:1-22)
  A. Report of the sign of the yoke (27:1-11)
  B. Oracle against false prophecy (27:12-15)
  C. Oracle against false prophecy (27:16-22)
III. Jeremiah's Confrontation with Hananiah (28:1-17)
  A. Hananiah disputes Jeremiah's prophecy (28:1-11)
  B. Oracle against Hananiah (28:12-17)

Jeremiah's Temple Sermon (26:1-24)
This sermon is reported in more detail in Jeremiah
7:1-15. Baruch perhaps wrote the summary in 26:1-6,
using parts of the sermon and other sayings from

Jeremiah (see Jeremiah 4:1-2; 18:7-11; 36:3). He was probably in the Temple with Jeremiah when Jeremiah deliverd this sermon.

Summary of the Sermon (26:1-6)

The beginning of Jehoiakim's reign was probably the fall of 609 B.C. The Feast of Booths, a harvest festival, was usually celebrated during the months of September/October. Many people from outlying areas came into Jerusalem and to the Temple at this time, so Jeremiah had a large audience for his sermon. At the temple gate, which is a small room allowing access through the wall, many people would be coming and going. This gate may be the one between the inner and outer courts in the temple area.

The message of Jeremiah's sermon is for the people of Israel, who are addressed as *the cities of Judah*. Jeremiah is not to hold back any part of his message. God understands that, despite Jeremiah's occasional anger and fear (for example, Jeremiah 18:18-23), Jeremiah often despairs of the message he must bring and would rather hold back.

The purpose of this sermon is to awaken repentance in the people (*listen . . . and turn*, verse 3). God will repent of evil if the people will repent of their evil. God is free to change in light of changes in the people (see also Amos 7:1-6). Because God's anger and punishment of the people of Israel are provoked by specific violations of the covenant (see Jeremiah 2:8), God's actions toward them will change if the people change their ways.

In general, to repent means to turn back, to renounce a given path. So, repentance is more than a feeling of being sorry for something and more than a change of mind. Repentance is an act of renewal involving the whole person. This is what Jeremiah says the people of Israel need.

A curse (verse 6) is an expression of an intention that

evil will befall a person or a place. Because of Israel's sin, God will make Jerusalem a source of evil and a place to be avoided (see also Jeremiah 18:16).

Report of Jeremiah's Arrest and Trial (26:7-24)

According to the law code in Deuteronomy, false prophets are to be put to death (Deuteronomy 18:20-22). On the basis of this law, the priests and prophets (who are probably official Temple prophets) bring charges against Jeremiah (verse 11). They do not want to wait to see if Jeremiah's words bear the test of time (see Deuteronomy 18:22). Their livelihoods are threatened by the possibility of the Temple being destroyed. The centralization of worship and sacrifice in the Jerusalem Temple by Josiah left them nowhere else to go. By this time in Israel's history, the priests had developed a virtual monopoly on the mechanics and economics of the worship and sacrificial ritual.

Priests are granted authority as judges and they hold court in the sanctuary. Elders of the people are also judges in certain cases and sit at the city gate to hear complaints and render judgments.

Jeremiah is brought before a group of princes (verse 10). These princes are not members of the royal family, but are officials of the king's court. They have authority to make a ruling in this case.

The exact location of the New Gate (verse 10) is not known. This may be the Benjamin Gate which is north of the Temple.

In his defense, Jeremiah repeats his prophecy (verses 12-13), then places himself at the mercy of the judges' decision. He declares his innocence by reminding the judges of the seriousness of shedding innocent blood (verse 15). Blood is sacred and is the source of life (see Deuteronomy 12:23). Blood that is shed in murder cries out to be avenged (see Genesis 4:10). The judges and all the people of Jerusalem will thus be bloodguilty if Jeremiah is killed (see Numbers 35:33).

The princes and the people declare their belief in what Jeremiah says (verse 16), though how may of these truly repent of their sins is not known. They may agree that Judah might be punished for her sins. However, they probably still believe that God will never allow Judah and the Temple to be destroyed.

The elders (verse 17) are older men who are local dignitaries or rulers. In defense of Jeremiah, one elder cites the precedent set by King Hezekiah (715–687 B.C.) in a case involving the prophet Micah. The quotation in verse 18 is from Micah 3:12.

Verses 20-24 tell of the prophet Uriah who is executed by Jehoiakim for prophesying the same judgment Jeremiah does. Baruch may place this account here in order to highlight the danger Jeremiah is in and to identify the official support that helps Jeremiah be acquitted.

Ahikam was an official in both Josiah's and Jehoiakim's administrations. His son Gedaliah was appointed governor of Judah by Nebuchadrezzar in 587 B.C. (see Jeremiah 40).

The *burial place* (verse 23) is a trench in the Kidron Valley east of Jerusalem where criminals and friendless foreigners are buried.

Report of the Sign of the Yoke (27:1-11)

The oracles in chapter 27 are from the beginning of the reign of King Zedekiah (597–587 B.C.). These oracles proclaim that the king of Babylon (called Nebuchadnezzar in chapters 27–29 instead of Nebuchadrezzar as elsewhere in Jeremiah) is God's ordained agent of punishment against all nations (verse 7).

The specific occasion for Jeremiah's sign act and related oracles in the presence of foreign envoys in Jerusalem (verse 3). Zedekiah and these envoys may be conspiring to combine their forces in a revolt against Babylon.

A revolt in Nebuchadnezzar's army (December 595–January 594 B.C.) and the ascension of a new Pharaoh (Psammetichus II, 594 B.C.) to the throne of Egypt may have stirred their hopes of getting out from under Babylonian control. Pro-Egyptian parties in Judah may have pushed such a move.

Jeremiah announces by sign and by word that rebellion is against God's will. The people of Israel must submit to Babylon or they will be cast out of their land (verse 10).

The straps and *bars* (verse 2) Jeremiah makes and wears are like those used on oxen. The bar is made of wood, and leather thongs that come down around the neck are attached to the bar.

Jeremiah associates false prophets with those who practice magic and divination (verse 9; see also Deuteronomy 18:10-12).

Oracle Against False Prophecy (27:12-15)

Jeremiah with the yoke on his neck stands before Zedekiah. He tells Zedekiah not to listen to the prophets who advise against serving Babylon. These prophets are unreliable because God has not sent them.

Zedekiah may have followed Jeremiah's counsel because Judah did not rebel at this time. Zedekiah was weak and in a precarious position having to please the Babylonians and the various factions within Judah. However, even he could probably see that Judah was in no shape to defy Babylon. Judah's territory had been reduced, some of her chief cities destroyed, her economy crippled, her population drastically reduced, and much of her leadership taken into exile.

Oracle About False Prophecy (27:16-22)

The false prophets discussed in this oracle are apparently official Temple prophets. Groups of prophets such as this are often attached to a shrine or sanctuary, to the Temple, or to the royal court. These kinds of prophets are frequently members of professional guilds who live and prophesy as a group, perhaps under the direction of a master.

The *vessels* (NRSV; NIV = articles) *of the Lord* are Temple equipment that was taken to Babylon as booty in 597 B.C. (see 2 Kings 24:13). Jeremiah says that those who prophesy a return of these treasures should instead pray that what they have left in the Temple will not also be taken.

The *pillars* are made of bronze and stand in front of the Temple (see 1 Kings 7:15-22).

The *sea* is a large bronze basin supported by twelve bronze oxen, which stands in the Temple court. This bronze basin holds about 12,000 gallons of liquid (see 1 Kings 7:25-26).

The *stands* (see 1 Kings 7:27-37) are highly ornamented bronze wagons on which wash basins are mounted.

The Babylonians wanted these items because of the value of the metal and because of their symbolic value. This symbolic value rests on the belief that to capture a people's gods, or their objects used in worship, is to capture their source of power.

Hananiah Disputes Jeremiah's Prophecy (28:1-11)

The beginning of Zedekiah's reign is qualified as the *fifth month of the fourth year*. This incident thus takes place in August of 594 B.C. Jeremiah is still wearing his yoke.

In the Temple, Hananiah speaks directly to Jeremiah. He contradicts Jeremiah's prophecy and breaks the yoke as a symbol of his own prophetic message (verses 2-4, 10-12).

Jeremiah does not angrily contradict Hananiah. Instead, Jeremiah says that he, too, would like to see victory and peace. He goes on, however, to remind Hananiah of the prophecies of their predecessors and of

the test of time required for proof of the truth (see also
Deuteronomy 18:20-22; Micah 3:5-12). Since the condition
and habits of the people of Israel are unchanged,
Jeremiah doubts the validity of Hananiah's promises.

Oracle Against Hananiah (28:12-17)

Sometime after Hananiah's actions and words to
Jeremiah in the Temple, the word of the Lord comes to
Jeremiah concerning this matter.

An iron yoke takes the place of the wooden yoke as the
symbol of Israel's servitude, though apparently Jeremiah
is not instructed to make and wear such a yoke.

Jeremiah announces a personal judgment on Hananiah
(verses 15-16). The legal basis for Hananiah's death
sentence is Deuteronomy 18:20-22. Hananiah's prophecy
is a rebellion against God's will for the people of Israel.

The oracles and narratives of chapters 26–28 testify
that prophecy, whether false or true, has its personal
risks for the prophet.

§ § § § § § §

The Message of Jeremiah 26–28

Jeremiah's message to the people of Israel at the beginning of the reign of Jehoiakim (609–598 B.C.) holds out the possibility of escape from punishment. God would "repent" if the people of Israel would "repent" (26:3). By the time of the reign of Zedekiah, however, the only alternative to destruction the people have is to serve the king of Babylon (27:8).

What has happened to bring about this change?

§ Neither the king nor many of the people listen to Jeremiah's warnings.

§ They recognize the power of his words but they do not believe his message and they want him out of the way.

§ False prophets and unreliable leaders continue to be a problem in Israel.

§ God expects the people to know a false prophet from a true one. The people are held responsible for choosing to believe lies rather than recognizing God's Word spoken by the true prophet.

§ The people have failed to recognize and obey the true Word. They must recognize and obey the Word even before the test of time has proven the Word.

§ § § § § § §

Jeremiah 29–31

Introduction to These Chapters

Chapter 29 continues the reports of Jeremiah's confrontations with religious leaders. The leaders named in this chapter are exiles living in Babylon.

Chapters 30–31 are often called *The Book of Consolation*. The oracles here deal with the future restoration of Israel and Judah.

Here is an outline of these chapters:
  I. Jeremiah's Letters to Babylon (29:1-32)
     A. Letter to the exiles (29:1-23)
     B. Jeremiah's dispute with Shemaiah (29:24-32)
 II. The Book of Consolation (30:1-31:40)
     A. The restoration of Israel and Judah (30:4–31:1)
     B. Oracles concerning future abundance (31:2-22)
     C. Oracles concerning the new covenant (31:23-40)

Jeremiah's Letters to Babylon (29:1-32)

Messages are exchanged between those people left in Jerusalem and those in exile. These letters are carried by royal couriers (verse 3) or by other travelers (see Ezekiel 33:21). To travel between Jerusalem and Babylon took from four to six months.

Letter to the Exiles (29:1-23)

The king's messengers take a letter from Jeremiah to the exile community living in Babylon. Zedekiah is perhaps sending his envoys to Nebuchadnezzar to assure the Babylonian king of his continued loyalty in the aftermath of possible plans for rebellion (see Jeremiah 27:3). Zedekiah himself visited Babylon in 593 B.C. (see Jeremiah 51:59). This visit may have been required by Nebuchadrezzar to reaffirm Zedekiah's loyalty to him. Some of the Israelite exiles may have been involved in the rebellion or in encouraging rebellion against Nebuchadrezzar in 595–594 B.C. (verses 7-8, 21).

King Jeconiah (verse 2) is Jehoiakim, who is still called the King of Judah by the Babylonians. His imprisonment by Nebuchadrezzar may have resulted from underground revolutionary activity that surrounded him in Judah and in Babylon.

Jeremiah delivers instructions from God to the exiles concerning their daily lives and their perspective on their captivity. The exiles are to make a home for themselves in Babylonia. They are to marry, have children, and multiply there, just as the Hebrews did during their slavery in Egypt. The exiles will find their well-being in Babylon's well-being because it is God's will for them to be there. Nebuchadrezzar is God's servant in regard to Israel.

Jeremiah condemns false prophets and magicians among the exiles who lead the people astray (verses 8-9). The exiles face the same conflicting prophecies as do those people left in Jerusalem. Each must discern the true prophetic word and abide by it.

The exiles do make homes for themselves in captivity. They build houses, grow food, and practice their various trades. Babylonian records from this time show payments in oil, barley, and other necessities to foreign captives in exchange for labor, though some captives are used as forced labor. Some Judeans work on construction projects for Nebuchadrezzar. The people are also allowed to assemble and to practice their religion. By 538 B.C., when they are officially allowed to return home, most of the exiles (now in their third generation in Babylon) choose to stay in their new homeland.

The exiles have to reassess their relationship to God. They are away from the Promised Land, from Jerusalem, and from the Temple. they can no longer go to the Temple for worship and sacrifice. Especially after the Temple is destroyed in 587 B.C., they are without that physical symbol and center of God's presence with them. Jeremiah tells them that their faith does not depend on living in the Promised Land nor on Temple sacrifices and ritual (as he does in Jeremiah 7:1-15, 21-22).

The one thing the exiles do have is the word of God. They can study the holy writings they brought with them. They can listen to and study the words of prophets like Jeremiah, Ezekiel, and Second Isaiah. In the exile, synagogue-type meetings are held for prayer and teaching. Through all this, the Israelites are on their way to becoming the people of the Word rather than strictly the people of a place (the Promised Land).

Verses 10-14 offer promises for the end of the Exile. God and Israel will then live in a new and mutually fulfilling relationship. Jeremiah assures the exiles that, even without the Temple and its ritual, God will meet them. They can offer themselves to God in their captivity, and God will see to their welfare.

Verses 16-19 break into the order of verses 15 and 20-23. This oracle is directed to those left in Jerusalem rather than to the exiles. It lets the exiles know what is going to happen to their kinsmen. An editor may have put these verses here, using language and images from some of Jeremiah's other prophecies.

Verses 15, 20-23 are a vehement oracle denouncing two prophets living in exile. The Babylonians would execute these men for political subversion rather than for the crimes Jeremiah lists.

Jeremiah must communicate more with the exile community than is indicated by the letters of chapter 29, since he knows such details about the private lives and prophecy of these two men.

Jeremiah's Dispute with Shemaiah (29:24-32)

Shemaiah, a prophet living in exile in Babylon, does not like what Jeremiah is writing to the exile community. He in turn writes letters to Jerusalem complaining about Jeremiah's prophecy. He wants to know why the priest in charge of the Temple has not disciplined Jeremiah and shut him up.

Zephaniah, the priest, reads this letter aloud in Jeremiah's hearing, Jeremiah then delivers an oracle which, first, repeats part of Shemaiah's letter (verses 25-28) as the reasons for punishment. Then it announces Shemaiah's punishment (verse 32).

Verse 24 should perhaps read *Concerning Shemaiah* because the oracle against him is delivered to the exile community in general. Most of Jeremiah's messages and announcements are spoken in the presence of more than one person. The community at large, either in Judah or in Babylon (through letters), shares in the message. This is because the message is not just for the individual concerned but also for the community. The purpose of prophecy includes teaching the people about what God is like and about God's will for them.

This larger perspective in prophecy is one reason the prophet's words are recorded and held to be of value to future generations. Jeremiah's words are directed to a particular community in a particular time, place, and circumstance. His words tell us about those people and what happened to them. They also teach us about God's nature and God's will. Jeremiah speaks of God's will concerning people in relationship to God and to one another. We, as well as the people who listened to Jeremiah, can learn about God through Jeremiah's words.

The Book of Consolation (30:1-31:40)

This book is a collection of oracles from different times in Jeremiah's ministry. Their theme is the restoration of the exiles to Palestine and the renewal of the relationship between God and the people of Israel. Israel and Judah are spoken of separately and as one people.

These oracles come in the middle of the biographical chapters (26-29; 32-45). They may have been put here because of their similarity to the restoration theme of Jeremiah 29:10-14. They also show a part of Jeremiah's prophecy that is different from the more numerous oracles of disaster. These oracles of hope complete Jeremiah's message and offer a perspective on the whole of God's plan for Israel.

Verses 30:1-3 are an introduction for the collection.

A *book* (verse 2) or scroll was written on strips of papyrus and then rolled up. A pen was made from a stalk of rush that was cut obliquely and then frayed at the end to form a brush. Ink was made from a mixture of soot or lampblack and gum arabic. The text was then written on the papyrus in columns with wide margins in between. Baruch probably wrote down Jeremiah's words in this way (Jeremiah 36:4).

The coming days of the Lord spoken of here will indeed be victorious for Israel. Israel will be healed and brought home; her enemies will be devoured. The people of Israel will not do this for themselves, however. All this will happen by God's will and by God's power. Israel may take comfort only in being chosen by God, not in her own accomplishments.

The Restoration of Israel and Judah (30:4-31:1)

This group of oracles has five parts:

(1) Verses 4-9: This oracle describes both judgment (verses 5-7) and freedom (verses 8-9). *That day* (verse 7) is God's day of judgment (see also Jeremiah 4:9; Amos 5:18-20). *That day* in verse 8 is a reversal of the conditions described in Jeremiah 25:14; 27:1-28:16.

Jacob means Israel. *David* means a king in the royal line of David (see Jeremiah 23:5-6).

(2) Verses 10-11: After a just punishment that the people deserve, God will bring them out of captivity.

(3) Verses 12-17: The two halves of this oracle, verses 12-15 and verses 16-17, do not fit smoothly together. Parts of two different oracles may be joined here to make the point that only God can restore Israel to health.

(4) *Verses* 18-22: This oracle describes the abundance and happiness of the restoration. The *mound* (NRSV; NIV = *ruins*) of the city refers to the practice of rebuilding on top of the rubble of a destroyed city. This practice produces the present-day flat-topped hills called *tells*.

The new ruler of Israel will be a combination prince and priest who will approach God in the Temple on the people's behalf.

Verse 21 may refer to the ritual in the Holy of Holies in the Temple. (See Exodus 33:20.) The phrase does not refer to persons seeking God in their own hearts (Jeremiah 29:12-14).

(5) *Verses* 30:23–31:1: Verses 23-24 are the same as Jeremiah 23:19-20. Verse 31:1 echoes the promise of 30:22.

Oracles Concerning Future Abundance (31:2-22)

These oracles may be divided as follows:

(1) *Verses* 2-6: In the coming great day for Israel, the watchmen will call the people, not to the alarms of war, but to worship in Jerusalem. The land and the people will be abundant under God's loving care.

The *wilderness* (NRSV, NIV = *desert*) recalls Israel's wandering after leaving Egypt. Israel found grace and favor with God in the wilderness through the covenant relationship.

Vineyards are planted on the sides of hills above the cultivated fields.

(2) *Verses* 7-14: God will gather the scattered flock of Israel, and from far and near the deliverance will be declared. Material and spiritual well-being will abound.

(3) *Verses* 15-22: This oracle promises that the northern tribes, who were overrun by Assyria in 722 B.C. and later by Babylon, will share in the restoration.

Rachel is the mother of Joseph and Benjamin and the ancestress of the northern tribes.

This particular *Ramah* is a town about five miles north of Jerusalem in the territory of Benjamin.

Road signs (NIV) or *road markers* (NRSV) remind the people of what led to their punishment and help them avoid such errors in the future (verse 21).

The exact meaning of verse 22b is uncertain. The Hebrew verb at the end of the sentence is variously translated in different versions of the Bible. In this saying, the *new thing* is perhaps that Israel (the *wife, daughter* in the covenant agreement) now turns to God (the *husband, father*) instead of to idols.

Oracles Concerning the New Covenant (31:23-40)

These oracles may be divided as follows:

(1) *Verses* 23-26: All of Judah will be restored. Verse 26 indicates that Jeremiah receives this oracle in a dream.

(2) *Verses* 27-28: This oracle reflects the promises of Jeremiah's commission to prophesy in Jeremiah 1:10.

(3) *Verses* 29-30: The proverb in this oracle reflects the belief in collective responsibility and collective retribution.

(4) *Verses* 31-34: These verses had great influence on the New Testament. They are quoted in Hebrews 8:8-12; 10:16-17, and are behind the words about the cup of the Lord's Supper in 1 Corinthians 11:25. The *new covenant* is referred to in other New Testament passages (for example, 2 Corinthians 3:5-6), and it influenced the distinction between the Old and New Testaments.

The new covenant is one of the inner being. The people's hearts, the wellsprings of human character, will be imprinted with the saving knowledge of God.

(5) *Verses* 35-40: This oracle promises that as long as the natural world lasts so will the people of Israel and Jerusalem. In verses 38-40, Jerusalem's four corners and southern and eastern boundaries are specified.

§ § § § § § §

The Message of Jeremiah 29–31

Jeremiah's messages to the people of Israel, both in Jerusalem and in exile, are not completely filled with promises of doom. The oracles in these chapters show that God's plans for Israel go beyond punishment to a more fulfilling future. What are these promises of hope?

§ The exile is not permanent. After seventy years the people will be able to go home.

§ In the meantime, they can live their normal lives in the confidence that God has not forgotten them.

§ Their new lives after their restoration will be fruitful and happy.

§ God's new covenant with them will bring an inward change and a new knowledge of God.

§ § § § § § §

Jeremiah 32–34

Introduction to These Chapters

These chapters pick up the biographical material on Jeremiah from chapter 29. The incidents and oracles here are from the time of Zedekiah.

Chapter 32 comes from 588/587 B.C. and tells of Jeremiah's purchase of land in Anathoth. Chapter 33 also comes from this time and is an appendix to the Book of Consolation. Chapter 34 comes from perhaps late 598 or early 588 B.C., near the time of or during the Babylonian siege of Jerusalem.

Here is an outline of these chapters:
I. Jeremiah's Purchase of a Field (32:1-44)
   A. Jeremiah buys the field (32:1-15)
   B. Jeremiah prays about the siege (32:16-25)
   C. God answers Jeremiah's prayer (32:26-44)
II. Appendix to the Book of Consolation (33:1-26)
III. Oracles to Zedekiah and to Jerusalem (34:1-22)
   A. Oracle to Zedekiah (34:1-7)
   B. Oracle concerning slavery in Jerusalem (34:8-22)

Jeremiah's Purchase of a Field (32:1-44)

Jeremiah's purchase of a field during the siege of Jerusalem illustrates his belief that Judah will eventually be redeemed. The prophet firmly believed that Judah would have a productive future as the oracles of chapters 30–31 declare. Jeremiah's action also is an example of the

91

application of the law of redemption of property (see Leviticus 25).

Jeremiah Buys the Field (32:1-15)

The *tenth year* of Zedekiah is late 588 or early 587 B.C. Chronologically, this account comes after Chapter 37. Jeremiah is arrested, perhaps because he attempts to leave the city (see Jeremiah 37:11-15). The *court of the guard* is an open court in the palace complex used to hold prisoners who do not require strict confinement. The word Jeremiah receives there concerns the purchase of family property.

The legal basis for Hanamel's request to Jeremiah is Leviticus 25:25. The purpose of the law and redemption is to allow families to maintain their property, and not let it pass to strangers or bill collectors. Hanamel may have financial problems because of the warfare in the land.

Jeremiah has the income to buy the land although the source of this income is not revealed. The account of the sale (verses 10-14) is the most detailed business transaction described in the Old Testament.

Seventeen shekels refers to the weight of the silver, which is about seven ounces.

The deed may be written in duplicate on a sheet of papyrus which is then cut in half. One copy is rolled and sealed and the open copy is attached to the sealed one. The papyrus may have been left in one piece with the top half rolled down and sealed and the bottom half left open. Such documents in sealed pottery jars have been found by archaeologists in Egypt and elsewhere.

The purchase of the land is a sign act (see also Jeremiah 13:1-11; 19:1-9; 27:1-7) that demonstrates Israel's future restoration (verse 15).

Jeremiah Prays About the Siege (32:16-25)

Jeremiah prays for insight into God's intentions concerning his purchase of the land. This is a formal prayer like those that might have been used in worship services. It praises God's infinite greatness (verses 17-19) and recounts God's mighty acts of the past (verses 20-23). Verse 24 describes conditions during the siege and 25 questions the land purchase in light of these conditions.

God Answers Jeremiah's Prayer (32:26-44)

God repeats the charges against Israel and Judah that have been declared before (verses 26-35), and repeats the promises of restoration under a new covenant (verses 36-41). The sign of the property purchase is explained as a demonstration that normal life and fortunes will return to the land (verses 42-44).

Appendix to the Book of Consolation (33:1-26)

Chapter 33 continues the themes taken up in chapters 30–31. Israel will be restored, healed, and brought to a new relationship with God. Verse 1 connects the chapter with chapter 32.

Verse 4 tells of the siege defense measures in which houses (perhaps those adjoining the city wall) are torn down (see also Isaiah 22:10).

God's *face* (verse 5), that is, God's benevolent presence, is turned away from Jerusalem.

Verses 6-26 shift to promises of restoration, health, prosperity, and security. Israel will be healed—will be mentally and physically well. Israel will be cleansed so that the inner stain and defilement of sin is removed. Israel will be forgiven so that the barriers between Israel and God are removed.

Jerusalem will gain renown, will gain a name for itself among the nations, not as a curse (see Jeremiah 26:6) but as a place of joy.

The conditions described in verse 10 are those suffered by Judah after the deportations of 587 B.C. and 582 B.C. The land was not entirely empty (as Jeremiah 40–44 tells), but the desolation was extensive. Archaeological evidence testifies that almost all the fortified towns in Judah were leveled and were not rebuilt for years to come. In addition to those people who were deported, thousands must have died in battle, of starvation, and of disease. Others fled to Egypt. The Babylonians did not bring in people from other parts of their empire to take the place of those deported or killed as the Assyrians had done in northern Israel. The Babylonians did not want Judah for what it could produce but rather for its strategic trade and military routes.

Some refugees may have drifted back to Judah after the fighting subsided. Though life was hard there, people harvested crops. Some pilgrims even went to the ruined Temple to offer sacrifices.

Verses 11-26 return to the promises of deliverance. The hymn of praise in verse 11 is also found in Psalm 136:1.

Verses 14-26 are a commentary on Jeremiah 23:5-6, which is paraphrased in verses 15-16. This commentary may be from the time of Haggai and Zechariah (520 B.C.) or the time of Malachi (500 B.C.) It may have been included in the collection of Jeremiah's works, because it quotes some of his words.

After the Exile, Judah did not achieve independence as a nation under Jewish ruler until 165 B.C.

Oracle to Zedekiah (34:1-7)

This oracle comes from a time when the actual siege of Jerusalem had not yet begun—perhaps late 589 B.C., or near the beginning of the siege in January 588 B.C.

At this stage of the Babylonian campaign, the only fortified cities that had not fallen were Jerusalem, Lachish, and Azekah. Lachish is twenty-three miles southwest of Jerusalem and Azekah is eleven miles north of Lachish. The Assyrians typically took the smaller towns of a country before attacking the capital. If the Babylonians followed this practice, then Jeremiah 34:1-7 may be from the months before Jerusalem was attacked, perhaps the summer of 589 B.C. Lachish was captured in the fall of 589 B.C.

Archaeological excavations at Lachish have found parts of letters written in Hebrew on broken pieces of pottery in the guard house at the entrance to the city. One such letter contains the words, "We are watching for the smoke signals of Lachish, according to all the indications which my lord gave, because we do not see Azekah." This letter was written to the commander at Lachish by the captain of an Israelite outpost within signaling distance of both Lachish and Azekah. The letter must have been written shortly after the fall of Azekah to the Babylonians, but before the fall of Lachish.

Jeremiah is not yet in prison. God sends him to Zedekiah with a warning about Jerusalem's coming destruction and his own captivity.

Zedekiah will have to face Nebuchadrezzar. Jeremiah assures him that he will die a peaceful death and receive funeral rites appropriate for a king. (See also 2 Chronicles 16:14.) This promise does not come to pass (compare Jeremiah 52:8-11). The promise may have had conditions attached to it, such as Zedekiah surrendering Jerusalem to the Babylonians (see Jeremiah 38:17), which are not mentioned here. The events described in Jeremiah 34:8-11 may have negated the promise (see also Jeremiah 34:21).

Oracle Concerning Slavery in Jerusalem (34:8-22)

Verses 8-11 tell about the slave owners in Jerusalem freeing their slaves and then changing their minds and taking the slaves back. Verses 12-22 are God's answer to their actions.

Exodus 21, Leviticus 25, and Deuteronomy 15 record Israelite laws concerning slavery. These laws are similar to those found in other legal codes of the ancient Near East. They define the rights and responsibilities of both slave and master in various cases.

Sources of slaves included captives of war and foreign

slaves imported into Israel by slave traders. Some people sold their children into slavery. Or, more commonly, they lost their children as slaves to creditors because the children had been put in pledge against unpaid debts. Hunger or debt also forced people to sell themselves into slavery. The majority of slaves were freeborn peple who were sold into slavery by their creditors because of bad debts. The term of service for such defaulting debtors was limited to six years. (See Exodus 21:2-4; Deuteronomy 15:12.)

Most slaves were owned by and worked in the households of the rich or of the nobility. Relatively few worked in agriculture or industry. This is because most of the arable land, except that owned by the crown or the Temple, was owned by and worked by freemen.

The Slaves Are Temporarily Freed

Sometime after the Babylonian siege of Jerusalem began in January of 588 B.C., the slave owners in the city made a covenant to release their Hebrew slaves, perhaps at Zedekiah's initiative. Their motives for this were probably mixed.

The slave owners were seeking God's favor by doing right in God's eyes. They were living up to the statutes in Exodus and Deuteronomy that are quoted in verse 14. Their fathers (and they) had not been freeing their slaves after six years as was required by law. (See also the charges of economic abuse made in Jeremiah 5:27-29.)

Also, the slave owners probably did not want the responsibility of feeding their slaves in a city suffering food shortages because of the siege. As freemen, the male slaves were also available for military service in defense of the city.

The Slaves Are Taken Back into Service

In the spring of 588 B.C., the Egyptian army came into Judah to help the Israelites. The Babylonians temporarily lifted the siege and moved to meet the approaching Egyptians (see verse 21).

The former slave owners take this to be a sign that Jerusalem is saved, so they take back their slaves. Apparently Zedekiah cannot or does not prevent them from doing this.

Punishment Is Announced

Jeremiah rebukes them for their breach of good faith (verses 12-22). The word *made*, used in relation to the covenant (verses 8, 13, 15), is literally cut. To *cut a covenant* is the oldest expression for covenant making. This term may come from the covenant ceremony itself. The details of verses 18-19 are similar to the ceremony described in Genesis 15:9-18.

The broken covenant is not only a transgression against those who are freed and enslaved again. The covenant to free the slaves was made in the Temple before God. Therefore, it carries the weight of God's name (verses 15). This covenant is a sacred agreement that has been broken.

Verse 22 proclaims that Nebuchadrezzar is still God's servant and will be brought back to conquer Jerusalem. God's covenant concerning the punishment of Jerusalem has not been broken.

§ § § § § § §

The Message of Jeremiah 32–34

In Jeremiah 32:27 God asks a question: "Behold, I am the Lord, the God of all flesh; is anything too hard for me?" Jeremiah shows that nothing is too hard for God and that God is free to work God's will in all of the earth.

§ In the midst of war and despair, God has Jeremiah purchase a field as a sign that Judah will one day be restored and productive.

§ In the midst of the false confidence and evil doings of the people and their leaders, God proclaims their punishment.

§ The masters of slaves in Jerusalem think they are in control and may take their slaves back into service as they please. They will discover, however, that God is a master greater than they are, and they will be punished for breaking their covenant with God.

§ In spite of all the terrible sins of the people of Israel, God declares that sin can be forgiven and that guilt can be cleansed.

§ § § § § § §

Jeremiah 35–37

Introduction to These Chapters

Chapter 35 tells how Jeremiah uses the Rechabites as a living sign concerning faithfulness to religious principles. Chapter 36 is an important source of information about the process by which Jeremiah's words and works were collected and written down. Chapter 37 begins the series of chapters that take Jeremiah from the siege of 587 B.C. through his prophecies in Egypt (chapters 37–44).

Chapters 35 (approximately 601 B.C.) and 36 (605–604 B.C.) are from the time of King Jehoiakim. Chapter 37 (588 B.C.) is from the time of King Zedekiah.

Here is an outline of these chapters:
  I. The Sign of the Rechabites (35:1-19)
 II. The Scroll of Jeremiah (36:1-32)
     A. Jeremiah's oracles written on a scroll (36:1-8)
     B. Baruch reads the scroll to the people (36:9-10)
     C. Baruch reads the scroll to the princes (36:11-19)
     D. The scroll is read to the king (36:20-26)
     E. Another scroll is made (36:27-32)
III. Jeremiah Is Arrested (37:1-21)
     A. Oracle to Zedekiah (37:1-10)
     B. Jeremiah is arrested and imprisoned (37:11-21)

The Sign of the Rechabites (35:1-19)
The historical background for chapter 35 is Jehoiakim's attempted rebellion against Babylon in 601 B.C. (See also

Jeremiah 12:7-13; 2 Kings 24:1-4.) After Babylonian forces suffered heavy losses in a battle with the Egyptians, Nebuchadrezzar withdrew to Babylon and spent a year reorganizing his army. Jehoiakim chose this opportunity to rebel, perhaps encouraged in this by the Egyptians. However, Nebuchadrezzar was not willing to let Judah go. He sent some Babylonian units as well as Arameans, Moabites, and Ammonites in raids against Judah. These raids forced people in the countryside to seek refuge in the fortified cities. Among the people coming into Jerusalem were the Rechabites. Jeremiah uses their presence to demonstrate the importance of loyalty to religious principles.

The Rechabites

The origins of the Rechabites are unknown. Biblical references to them give few clues about where they came from or who founded the group. They may be related to the Kenites, a nomadic desert-dwelling people who allied themselves with the Israelites during the days of the judges (see Judges 4–5). The Rechabites were active in the campaign of Jehu (King of Israel, 842–815 B.C.) against Ahab and Jezebel and all forms of pagan worship. (See 2 Kings 10:15-28.)

Rechabites lived in tents, not houses. They were shepherds, not farmers, and they refused to drink wine. Their way of life supported their belief that Israel's true worship of God was found in their desert-dwelling days. The Rechabites condemned the pagan influences Israel gave in to when the people of Israel settled into agricultural life in Canaan. Since grape culture and wine-making were not practiced by nomads, wine became a symbol to the Rechabites of the corruptions found in settled life in Canaan.

When the Rechabites came to Jerusalem for protection against the raiders, they may have continued to live in their tents inside the city walls. They condemned settled life in walled cities but they had to seek refuge there. They were caught in a situation where they had to seek protection from people whose lifestyle they protested. God instructs Jeremiah to use this situation to make a point about faithfulness.

Jeremiah and the Rechabites

Jeremiah gathers the Rechabites in a chamber of the Temple. Such a gathering would attract the attention of Israelites who are in the Temple area and who would be curious enough to watch and listen to Jeremiah's dialogue with the Rechabites.

Chambers (NRSV; NIV = *side rooms*) are meeeting room or perhaps storerooms or residences within the Temple complex.

Jeremiah places wine before the Rechabites andd tells them to drink, knowing that they will refuse. Their reply to Jeremiah's request (verses 6-11) provides the basis for the oracles that follow in verses 12-19.

The first oracle (verses 12-17) is addressed to *the men of Judah and the inhabitants of Jerusalem.* This oracle interprets the meaning of the demonstration Jeremiah sets up with the Rechabites. He asks the people if they cannot follow God's instructions as well as the Rechabites follow the instructions of their founder. They are true to their beliefs in order to *live many days in the land* (verse 7). God wants the people of Israel to turn away from evil so that they may *live in the land* (verse 15). But Israel refuses to listen and to obey.

The people of Israel have forgotten that they, like the Rechabites, are considered to be sojourners in the land. In the Old Testament, a sojourner is someone who lives in a foreign land at the hospitality of the natives or owners of the land. Sojourners are not natives, but neither are they considered to be foreigners. The people of Israel are sojourners in the Promised Land and also in God's favor.

The Israelites enjoy God's hospitality as long as they

live as God's people. (See also Leviticus 25:23; Deuteronomy 6:10-12, 20-25; Psalm 39:12; 119:19.)

Verses 18-19 are an oracle addressed to the Rechabites which is spoken in the presence of the Israelites. The blessing promised the faithful Rechabites contrasts sharply with the punishment promised the Israelites.

Verse 19 means that Jonadab will be blessed with descendants who will continue to serve the Lord.

Jeremiah's use of the Rechabites as an object lesson does not mean that he favors a nomadic lifestyle over a settled one. Nor does it mean that he believes people should not drink wine. However, Jeremiah does point to Israel's days of wandering in the wilderness as a time of fidelity to the covenant. Jeremiah 2:2-3 recalls this stage of Israel's history as one of devotion to God. Even in these verses, however, illustrations drawn from nomadic life and settled life are mixed. Israel found God in *a land not sown* but also was as the *first fruit of harvest* to God.

The point is that Jeremiah calls the people to faithfulness, whether they live in houses or tents, and whether they are farmers or shepherds.

The Scroll of Jeremiah (36:1-32)

In 605 B.C. Jeremiah dictates to Baruch *all the words* he has received from God since the days of Josiah. The writing of the scroll may be prompted by Babylon's advance against Egypt at Carchemish and Hamath in the spring and summer of 605 B.C. Judah, which had been under Egyptian control since 609 B.C., is now in danger (see Jeremiah 25:1-14).

The Babylonian advance was halted for a time when Nebuchadrezzar's father died and Nebuchadrezzar returned to Babylon to be crowned king. Nebuchadrezzar resumed his military campaigns in 604 B.C. and moved against the Philistines on Judah's doorstep. By 603 B.C. Jehoiakim transferred his allegiance from Egypt to Babylon and became Nebuchadrezzar's vassal.

Jeremiah's Oracles Written on a Scroll (36:1-8)

Jeremiah is barred from the Temple, perhaps because his previous speeches there have angered the priests. (See, for example, Jeremiah 7:1-8.)

Jeremiah sends Baruch to the Temple on a fast day when many people from outside Jerusalem are gathered there. The fast and ceremonies accompanying it may be intended to seek God's favor and to ask for deliverance from the threat posed by the Babylonians. Or, perhaps the people want to seek deliverance from drought.

Baruch is Jeremiah's companion and scribe. The Jewish historian Josephus (A.D. 37–100) describes Baruch as being from a very distinguished family and exceptionally well instructed in his native tongue. Baruch is entrusted with what may be the first public reading of portions of the Book of Jeremiah.

Baruch Reads the Scroll to the People (36:9-10)

The *fifth* year is 605–604 B.C., since Jehoiakim became king in the fall of 609 B.C. The *ninth month* of the Hebrew calendar is December because the year begins in the spring. Jeremiah may have dictated the scroll in the fall of 605 B.C., late in Jehoiakim's fourth year as king. Baruch may have read it in the Temple in December of 605 B.C., early in Jehoiakim's fifth official year as king (or possibly in December of 604 B.C.)

Verses 8 and 10 may refer to the same reading.

Baruch Reads the Scroll to the Princes (36:11-19)

The secretary (verse 12) is a royal scribe who is in charge of the royal archives and correspondence.

The princes are leading government officials. They anticpate Jehoiakim's displeasure with Jeremiah's words.

The Scroll Is Read to the King (36:20-26)

Jehoiakim ignores the warnings of the scroll and displays his contempt by burning it. Through the foresight of the princes and with God's help (verses 19, 26) Jeremiah and Baruch escape Jehoiakim's wrath.

Another Scroll Is Made (36:27-32)

Jeremiah announces an oracle against Jehoiakim and his follower (verses 29-31), and then dictates another copy of his words to Baruch (verse 32). The king's threats do not stop Jeremiah's prophecy.

Jeremiah Is Arrested (37:1-21)

Chapter 37 continues the reports of Jeremiah's trials and tribulations, but it moves ahead to the spring of 588 B.C. This is about the same time as the events reported in Jeremiah 34. Zedekiah is king and has given in to those in Jerusalem who have been plotting rebellion against Babylon. Jerusalem is under siege, though the city is enjoying a temporary reprieve. The Babylonians have withdrawn to meet advancing Egyptian forces.

Oracle to Zedekiah (37:1-10)

Zedekiah sends a delegation asking Jeremiah to interceded with God for Judah. Jeremiah is to *inquire* of God (verse 7), since part of his prophetic duty is to mediate between God and the people. As an answer, Zedekiah receives a message of doom.

Jeremiah Is Arrested and Imprisoned (37:11-21)

Jeremiah tries to take advantage of the lull in fighting to travel to Anathoth, in the land of Benjamin. Jeremiah had been encouraging the people of Jerusalem to surrender to the Babylonians (see Jeremiah 21:8-9), and he is arrested for alleged desertion.

The princes (verse 14) are not the same men as the princes of chapter 36. The princes of Jehoiakim had been taken into exile in 598 B.C. Zedekiah's princes do not want to surrender to Babylonian rule. They beat Jeremiah and throw him in a dungeon.

Zedekiah secretly sends for Jeremiah and again asks for a word from God. The word is not good (verse 17). Jeremiah points out the obvious error of the prophets who had promised peace and victory for Judah. But Zedekiah still does not follow Jeremiah's message.

Zedekiah is afraid of the princes and goes along with them even though events have proven Jeremiah correct. Zedekiah is surrounded by enemies, with the Babylonians on one side and his rebellious princes (who still consider Jehoiakim their true king) on the other. His only true source of help is in following God's instructions given through Jeremiah. But he is afraid to trust God's Word.

Zedekiah does stand up to the princes enough to transfer Jeremiah from the dungeon to the court of the guard (32:2). He also sees that Jeremiah is fed.

§ § § § § § §

The Message of Jeremiah 35–37

The oracles and events of chapters 35–37 show that God's Word will survive and will be confirmed.

§ In the midst of rebellious and unfaithful Jerusalem, Jeremiah finds the Rechabites. Their lives are living, daily testimony to their faith and their tradition. They are an example to Israel of faithfulness to religious principles.

§ Even though the king burns the record of Jeremiah's words, another scroll is made. God's Word through Jeremiah has survived to this day.

§ History bears out the true prophetic word.

§ God watches over Jeremiah so that Jeremiah may continue to proclaim God's Word to Israel.

§ § § § § § §

Jeremiah 38–40

Introduction to These Chapters

Chapters 38–40 continue the story of Jerusalem under siege and tell what happens to Jeremiah after the city falls. In chapter 38, Jeremiah is almost killed by Zedekiah's advisors who favors the rebellion against Babylon. Chapter 39 describes the fall of Jerusalem. Chapter 40 begins a narrative (chapters 40–41) that reports on Jeremiah's relationship to the governor of Judah appointed by Nebuchadrezzar in 587 B.C.

Here is an outline of these chapters:
I. Jeremiah Insists on Surrender (38:1-28)
  A. Jeremiah in the cistern (37:1-13)
  B. Oracles to Zedekiah (38:14-28)
II. The Fall of Jerusalem (39:1-18)
  A. Report of defeat and exile (39:1-10)
  B. Jeremiah and the Babylonians (39:11-18)
III. Gedaliah Appointed Governor (40:1-16)
  A. Jeremiah remains with Gedaliah (40:1-6)
  B. Report of Gedaliah's administration (40:7-16)

Jeremiah Insists on Surrender (38:1-28)
Hopes for Egypt's help are still high in Jerusalem, at least among some of the palace officials. However, they are not confident enough to tolerate Jeremiah's announcements of defeat and messages advocating surrender.

Jeremiah in the Cistern (38:1-13)

The oracle in verses 2-3 announces judgment in the same terms as in Jeremiah 21:9-10. The officials listed in verse 1 go to Zedekiah to persuade him that Jeremiah is weakening the war effort by his prophecy (verse 4). Zedekiah gives in to them and admits his own helplessness.

The cistern is a pit that catches rainwater and stores it for use during the dry summer months. Israelite cisterns typically have a bottle-shaped reservoir with a narrow opening at the top which is sometimes covered with a large flat stone. The reservoir is cut into rock and lined with a lime plaster. Since the cistern is nearly dry, this incident must have taken place sometime in the summer, probably the summer of 587 B.C. before Nebuchadrezzar's final assault on Jerusalem.

Jeremiah had been confined in the court of the guard the previous year (see Jeremiah 37:11-21). He may have been released when food supplies ran short (see 37:21). He may have continued in confinement but also may have continued his prophetic announcements. Perhaps he addressed his fellow prisoners or their visitors.

Jeremiah is rescued from the cistern by an Ethiopian who is an important palace official. This Ethiopian is not necessarily a eunuch physically, because the Hebrew word translated *eunuch* may simply mean *palace official.* He confronts Zedekiah with the evil the king has allowed against Jeremiah and wins the king's approval to rescue the prophet.

The Benjamin Gate is in the north wall of the city. Zedekiah may be sitting there hearing legal cases or may be observing the fighting.

Jeremiah is pulled out of the cistern but he remains in the court of the guard. He must have some freedom of movement within the palace grounds, however, for God instructs him to speak an oracle of deliverance to Ebedmelech (Jeremiah 39:15-18). Ebedmelech's life is saved because his efforts to rescue Jeremiah demonstrate his trust in God.

That a foreigner rescues Jeremiah and is rewarded for his actions highlights the wickedness of Jeremiah's fellow Israelites in trying to murder him. This story also illustrates Jeremiah's hope that all nations will one day come to God (see Jeremiah 3:17).

Oracles to Zedekiah (38:14-28)

Zedekiah meets secretly with Jeremiah asking for Jeremiah's counsel. The exact location of the *third entrance* is not known, but it is probably a gate between the Temple and the palace. Jeremiah is understandably suspicious because of his previous treatment, but Zedekiah swears to Jeremiah's safety.

Jeremiah repeats his counsel of *surrender and live, fight and die*. (See also Jeremiah 20:1-6; 21:4-10; 27:1-11.) Zedekiah voices his fears of reprisals from Jews who have already surrendered (see Jeremiah 39:9; 52:15). In response to Zedekiah's fears, Jeremiah tells him about a vision. In the vision, members of Zedekiah's own household recite a poem of lamentation over Zedekiah's defeat.

Zedekiah still hestitates to listen to Jeremiah's warnings. He gets Jeremiah to agree to keep their conversation a secret and returns Jeremiah to house arrest.

Report of Defeat and Exile (39:1-10)

These verses summarize the account of the siege found in Jeremiah 52:4-16 (see also 2 Kings 25:1-12). The names of Babylonian officials are added in verse 3.

The Siege

The Babylonians probably focused their attack on the north wall of the city. The slope of the land leading up to the north wall is gentle, but it is steep on the other sides.

The Babylonians also probably followed strategies of attack that were typical of siege warfare at this time in history.

A siege was generally begun by the attackers filling in any moats or ditches lying across their approach to a city. The attackers also built ramps to reduce the slope of their attack. Also, these ramps allowed wheeled battering rams and towers for archers to be moved into position close to the walls of the city.

Rock and dirt were brought in for fill and wooden tracks for the rams and towers were constructed on the ramps. The wood came from trees cut down near the city (see, for example, Jeremiah 6:6). Such construction work was dangerous because of the stones and arrows hurled from the walls by the defenders of the city. Shield-bearers provided some protection for the construction workers. Siegeworks or mounds of dirt may also have been built as protection from archers.

When the ramps were ready, battering rams were moved into place against the walls and gates, and the attack began. In support of the battering ram crews, archers and slingmen aimed arrows and stones against the defenders on the towers and walls of the city. This action made it hard for the defenders to concentrate their counterattack on the rams. They tried to disable the rams using chains and grapnels. Catapults may have been used behind the front line to sling stones and fire against and over the walls.

The defenders sought protection behind the tops of the walls and behind arrangements of shields in their counterattack. Nevertheless, the rams, the archery towers, and the access to food and water favored the attackers.

Near the end of June 587 B.C., the Babylonian forces breached the double wall on the north side of Jerusalem. Part of the wall may have given way or perhaps one of the gates gave in under the pounding of a battering ram. The assault troops then concentrated their attack on the weak point. Scaling ladders were set up against the walls. Troops armed with swords and spears raced up the ladders while the defenders poured boiling oil on them or rained down stones and arrows. The assault troops gradually made it over the top while more pressed through the opening made in the wall. At that point, the defenders had lost.

In that way, Babylonian forces took Jerusalem after eighteen months of backbreaking labor and bloodshed on both sides.

After the Babylonians entered Jerusalem, Zedekiah escaped through an unguarded gate in the north wall of the city. He headed into the desert area that borders Jerusalem on the east (verse 4).

According to Jeremiah 52:4-16, Jerusalem was sacked and burned in August of 587 B.C., one month after its capture.

Jeremiah and the Babylonians (39:11-18)

The Babylonians may have heard of Jeremiah from the Israelites who surrendered before Jerusalem fell. Jeremiah was released from confinement into the custody of Gedaliah, who was appointed Judah's new governor (Jeremiah 40:5). (See "Jeremiah in the Cistern," 38:1-13, regarding verses 15-18.)

Jeremiah Remains with Gedaliah (40:1-6)

This report, which says that Jeremiah is first taken to Ramah, a transit point for deportees, and then released to Gedaliah, is difficult to understand after reading 39:11-14. Verses 1-6 may be from a different, perhaps later, account of what happened to Jeremiah after the siege.

Verse 1 announces *the word that came to Jeremiah from the Lord,* but no oracles or speeches from Jeremiah are recorded. In fact, Jeremiah is not mentioned in any of the material from 40:7-41:18. The *word* of verse 1 may refer to the speech made by the Babylonian officer to Jeremiah in verses 2-5. Jeremiah is given special treatment and is allowed to choose between exile and residence in Judah. Jeremiah chooses to stay in his homeland. His previous pleas to the people of Jerusalem to submit to Babylon were not made out of disloyalty to his country. They were based on the conviction that Israel must submit to God's will.

Jeremiah chooses to stay among the poor people who will struggle to make a living in the depleted land (see also Lamentations 5:1-18). He also stays to proclaim God's word to the leaders of the people who are left (see Jeremiah 42:1-5).

Report of Gedaliah's Administration (40:7-16)

Judah is organized as a province of the Babylonian empire and Gedaliah is appointed governor. Gedaliah is a member of a promiment Judean family whose father, Ahikam, had been an official in the courts of King Josiah and King Jehoiakim. Ahikam had come to Jeremiah's aid in 609 B.C. (see Jeremiah 26:24).

Gedaliah was a chief palace administrator under Zedekiah. A seal from this time that read "Gedaliah who is over the house" was discovered in archaeological excavations at Lachish. Gedaliah may also have been appointed governor because he was not inclined to lead another rebellion against the Babylonians.

Gedaliah's administration lasts about five years until his assassination by zealous Israelites patriots (see Jeremiah 41:1-2). According to Jeremiah 52:30, the Babylonians deport more Israelites from Judah in 582–581 B.C. This deportation is probably in retaliation for disturbances related to the assassination.

Gedaliah sets up his provincial government in Mizpah, north of Jerusalem in the territory of Benjamin. Israelites who had been in hiding from the Babylonians come to receive his instructions (verses 7-8, 11-12). He encourages them to settle down and resume their normal lives once more. He promises to speak on their behalf to the representatives of Nebuchadrezzar who oversee the Babylonian king's territories. Gedaliah tells the people what Jeremiah has been telling them—serve Babylon and live (verse 9).

Gedaliah's years as governor are not entirely bad for the people. There is at least one good harvest (reported in verse 12) and possibly more. Some pilgrims feel secure enough to travel to Jerusalem to the site of the Temple ruins (see Jeremiah 41:4).

Peace in the land, a chance to plant and harvest, and a chance to take care of their families are not enough for everyone, however. Some Israelites still rebel against God's ordained punishment. They will not agree to serve the Babylonians and they bring bloodshed back to Judah (Jeremiah 41).

§ § § § § § §

The Message of Jeremiah 38–40

God's promises of defeat for Israel are realized as the Babylonians take Jerusalem in 587 B.C. By this time Jeremiah has been prophesying for about forty years. During this time he has suffered physical abuse and mental and emotional anguish. What does Jeremiah do as his announcements of punishment for Israel are fulfilled?

§ In spite of continued threats and abuse, Jeremiah still proclaims the unpopular message of punishment.

§ He continues to offer hope to those who submit to God's judgment and trust in God.

§ He chooses to stay in his ruined homeland. His duties to Israel are not over because he continues to care for the welfare of his people.

§ § § § § § §

PART
FOURTEEN **Jeremiah 41–45**

Introduction to These Chapters

These chapters take Jeremiah from his defeated homeland into unwilling exile in Egypt. After Gedaliah's assassination (chapter 41), the commanders of the remaining Israelite forces come to Jeremiah and seek a word from God through him (chapter 42). They decide not to obey Jeremiah's message but rather flee to Egypt taking Jeremiah with them. In Egypt, Jeremiah continues his prophecy (chapter 44). The prophecies against Israel end with a look back at God's promises of difficulties and of deliverance (chapter 45).

Here is an outline of chapters 41–45:
I. Report of Gedaliah's Murder (41:1-18)
   A. Gedaliah and others are killed (41:1-3)
   B. Some pilgrims are spared (41:4-9)
   C. Ishmael escapes (41:10-18)
II. The Flight to Egypt (42:1-43:7)
   A. The people seek an oracle (42:1-6)
   B. Jeremiah warns against Egypt (42:7-22)
   C. Jeremiah taken to Egypt (43:1-7)
III. Sign Act Against Egypt (43:8-13)
IV. Israel's Idolatry in Egypt (44:1-30)
   A. Oracle against the refugees (44:1-14)
   B. Oracle against idolatry (44:15-30)
V. Oracle to Baruch (45:1-5)

Gedaliah and Others Are Killed (41:1-3)

The *seventh month* is September/October, possibly in 582 B.C. One of Gedaliah's commanders tells him of a plot on his life. But Gedaliah does not believe the report (see Jeremiah 40:13-16), possibly because Ishmael had earlier sworn allegiance to him (see 40:8).

Ishmael is a member of the royal family who wants no accommodation with the Babylonians. He takes refuge from the Babylonians in Ammon. Ammon had been in revolt against Babylonian domination since the days of Zedekiah (see Jeremiah 27:3). Nebuchadrezzar had not yet crushed them as he had Judah. The king of Ammon collaborates with Ishmael to kill Gedaliah in hopes of taking control of all or part of Judah. Though the attack on Gedaliah is successful (41:2), the Babylonians retaliate against both Judah and Ammon. As a result, settled life in Ammon virtually ended for the next 300 years.

Gedaliah should have listened to the warnings of Johanan. With Gedaliah's death, the Jews remaining in Judah (the remnant of Jeremiah 40:15) are further scattered.

Some Pilgrims Are Spared (41:4-9)

Pilgrims from the north are unwittingly caught in Ishmael's deadly plot. Shechem, Shiloh, and Samaria are cities that were once part of the Northern Kingdom but had been taken into Judah during the reign of Josiah.

The eighty men are in mourning (verse 5) and are on their way to Jerusalem to present their offerings at the Temple. By this time, some rituals of worship and sacrifice had been resumed at the Temple site.

No reason is given for Ishmael's pleading with them to come into Mizpah and then killing all of them except the ten. If he killed them to keep his previous murders a secret, then he probably would not have spared even the ten.

The food these men used to bargain for their lives is

their offering for the Temple and perhaps also their food for travel. If food is in short supply in Judah, Ishmael may need this food to sustain his guerilla band.

Ishmael's plans and motives are not clear from this report. However, it is clear that he is ruthless and zealous in his cause.

King Asa was a Judean king (see 1 Kings 15:22).

Ishmael Escapes (41:10-18)

Prompt action by Johanan saves the captives Ishmael is taking to Ammon, though Ishmael himself escapes.

Gibeon is approximately two miles northeast of Mizpah.

Geruth Chimham perhaps means *Chimham's Inn.* It is near Bethelem, south of Jerusalem.

Jeremiah and Baruch may be among the captives who are rescued (see Jeremiah 40:6), but no record of them from this time has survived. Jeremiah is surely grieved about the murders and alarmed at what this will mean for Judah.

The Flight to Egypt (42:1-43:7)

Johanan and the other commanders are naturally concerned that Nebuchadrezzar will think they are part of Ishmael's rebellion. They immediately head for Egypt, then have second thoughts and appeal to Jeremiah for guidance.

The People Seek an Oracle (42:1-6)

The leaders of the small Israelite band ask Jeremiah to intercede with God for them. One of Jeremiah's responsibilities as a prophet to his people is to seek God's word on their behalf. (See also Jeremiah 21:1-2; 37:3.) They must decide whether to risk remaining in Judah to try to prove their innocence and their obedience to Nebuchadrezzar. If they leave Judah for Egypt, they will be further from Nebuchadrezzar's grasp. But they will also be open to charges that they are guilty of rebellion and murder. Egypt, after all, had sided with Judah against Babylon in the past.

Despite their assurances to Jeremiah that they will abide by his word (verses 5-6), they must harbor doubts about God's purposes for them. Jeremiah had been telling them to accept the Babylonians as their masters, at least temporarily. Most of them had done so after Jerusalem was destroyed. They had been loyal to Gedaliah, Babylon's appointed ruler. After he is murdered they naturally are suspects.

Gedaliah's death may have profoundly shaken their confidence that God is indeed planning their welfare and not their destruction. Their faith is once again severely tested.

Jeremiah Warns Against Egypt (42:7-22)

After ten days of prayer and reflection, Jeremiah brings the people an answer (verses 9-12). This may be a difficult time for Jeremiah, in which he struggles to be sure he correctly understands God's will on the issue of staying in Judah or going to Egypt.

Jeremiah himself had pointed out before the fall of Jerusalem that residence in Judah is, in and of itself, no guarantee of God's favor. In his letter to the exiles (Jeremiah 29:1-9), Jeremiah advises them to settle down, raise families, and get on with their lives because God is with them even in a foreign land.

However, Jeremiah does affirm that life will go on in Judah and will one day resume its normal dimensions (see Jeremiah 32:6-15). Gedaliah's instructions to the people remaining in Judah are also aimed at restoring the routines of family and agriculture (see Jeremiah 40:9-10).

The question of whether to go to Egypt or stay in Judah cannot be answered easily or quickly.

Verses 13-22 (particularly verses 18-21) anticipate the leader's refusal to obey Jeremiah's message. Perhaps this part of Jeremiah's answer should be placed between

Jeremiah 43:3 and 43:4 as a response to the rejection of his counsel.

Jeremiah probably hears the people discuss their situation among themselves during the days they wait for Jeremiah's answer. They are tired of war and tired of struggling to feed themselves. Egypt offers the promise of a respite from war and of food for their children.

However, Egypt had promised Judah help in the past against the Babylonians and had only led Judah further away from God's will. Egypt never failed to take advantage of Judah for her own benefit, either. Though the bread basket of the Nile had provided food for hungry Israelites in the past, Jeremiah declares that the remnant of Judah will find only suffering there now.

Jeremiah Taken to Egypt (43:1-7)

The leaders decide against Jeremiah. They insolently accuse Jeremiah of lying to them under Baruch's influence. Though no evidence is given for their accusations, they do seem to indicate that Jeremiah and Baruch are close friends as well as master and scribe. The leaders are fearful of what Nebuchadrezzar may do to them because of the murders, more fearful than they are of disobeying God's word. They rationalize their disobedience by slandering Jeremiah and Baruch.

The commanders force Jeremiah and Baruch into exile. They do this to keep them from talking to the Babylonians or perhaps to have Jeremiah available for future intercession with God. King Zedekiah also repeatedly sought Jeremiah's word from God even though he did not follow it. Like Zedekiah, the leaders of Jeremiah's group allow their fear to guide them instead of allowing God to guide them.

Sign Act Against Egypt (43:8-13)

Tahpanhes is a fortress city on the Egyptian border in the eastern part of the Nile Delta.

Jeremiah performs a sign act to demonstrate that Egypt is no refuge from Nebuchadrezzar. The stones Jeremiah set up are a symbolic base for Nebuchadrezzar's throne that will sit over the stone and under the royal tent. *Pharaoh's palace* (verse 9) is probalby a government building rather than a royal residence.

Nebuchadrezzar is God's servant, God's agent of punishment. He can reach wherever God's will directs him to reach. The purposes and power of God are not confined to the Promised Land. This is an important lesson for the exiles in Egypt and in Babylon to learn.

The Babylonians raided Egypt in 568/567 B.C. and possibly also in 582/581 B.C. Though Egypt maintained her independence, the Babylonians were clearly the master power in the ancient Near East at this time.

Oracle Against the Refugees (44:1-14)

Jeremiah addresses all the Jews living in Egypt. Though they all are not within the sound of his voice, his declaration of God's word for them still has creative power to accomplish God's will. Even those Jews in distant cities probably had word of Jeremiah's prophecy. We know that the colonies of exiles stayed in communication with one another.

Jeremiah reminds the people of past mistakes and warns them of the consequences of continuing sin and disobedience (similar to Jeremiah 42:14-22).

Oracle Against Idolatry (44:15-30)

The refugees reply to Jeremiah that they are better off when they worship the *queen of heaven*. This queen is the goddess Ishtar, the goddess of Venus. This fertility goddess is served with special devotion by some Jewish women. Jeremiah reminds the exiles of what happened to Judah because of idolatry. In the relative comfort of Egypt, however, they do not care.

Verses 29-30 offer the Jews a sign that their

punishment will follow them into Egypt. Hophra was Pharaoh of Egypt from 588-569 B.C. He sent an army to aid Judah in 588 B.C. against the Babylonians (see Jeremiah 37:5). He was assassinated in 569 B.C. by Amasis (Ahmosis II) who was Pharaoh from 569-526 B.C.

Exile in Egypt offers Jeremiah no rest from his duties of declaring God's judgment to the disobedient people of Israel.

Oracle to Baruch (45:1-5)

This oracle is dated in 605 B.C. Baruch has voiced his fears and concerns to God and God answers him in this oracle. God's reply is similar in tone to the replies given to Jeremiah's sorrows (see Jeremiah 12:5; 15:19). In the face of Baruch's woes, God offers a mild rebuke and a reminder of God's larger purposes that are at work in Baruch. Baruch is assured of his life and of God's care.

§ § § § § § §

The Message of Jeremiah 41–45

The oracle in Jeremiah 45:2-5 comes at the end of the long narrative about Jeremiah's life and ministry (chapters 26–45). This oracle helps to put the lives of God's servants into perspective.

§ The book of Jeremiah shows that, from the beginning of Jeremiah's life to the end, God's message to Israel is put before personal considerations.

§ Though prophets, kings, or ordinary people may desire "great things," God's purposes are the only truly great things.

§ God's purposes will always be accomplished.

§ § § § § § §

Jeremiah 46–49

Introduction to These Chapters

Chapters 46–49 are a collection of oracles against nations other than Israel. Some of the nations addressed in these oracles are also listed in the oracle in Jeremiah 25:19-26. Jeremiah 25:19-38 may have introduced the collection of oracles in chapters 46–49 at one stage in the collection of Jeremiah's work.

The oracles themselves have few references to historical events and they do not mention specific kings (though the introductions in 46:2, 13 and 47:1 do give some historical references). The collection may not have been included in the scroll of Jeremiah's words that was made by Baruch. A later collector may have brought these oracles together. At some time in the editorial process, the colleciton was put at the end of Jeremiah's memoirs.

Unlike Jeremiah's oracles against Israel, the oracles in chapters 46–51 contain verses apparently borrowed from other Old Testament books, especially Isaiah and Obadiah. So parts of these oracles may have come from a later writer rather than from Jeremiah.

The nations are soundly condemned to punishment, but Egypt, Moab, Ammon, and Elam are promised future restoration. The *day of the* LORD (see Jeremiah 25:33; 46:10) is a day of defeat for other nations as well as for Israel. All flesh must drink the cup of God's wrath. This is not accomplished in one twenty-four hour day. Each nation in turn feels the consequences of God's judgment. Each has *magnified* itself against God, has set itself against God's purposes, and has trusted in power and riches. Even Babylon, who deals out God's punishment to Israel and to these others, will face judgment (chapters 50–51). The prophetic message is always that human might must give way to God. Those in power are brought low, and the death they dealt to others is dealt to them as God's purposes are worked out in human history.

Here is an outline of chapters 46–49:
  I. Oracles Against Egypt (46:1-28)
    A. Oracle to Pharaoh's army (46:2-12)
    B. Oracle about Nebuchadrezzar in Egypt (46:13-26)
    C. Consolation for Israel (46:27-28)
  II. Oracle Against the Philistines (47:1-7)
  III. Oracles Against Moab (48:1-47)
  IV. Oracle Against the Ammonites (49:1-6)
  V. Oracle Against Edom (49:7-22)
  VI. Oracle Against Damascus (49:23-27)
  VII. Oracle Against Kedar and Hazor (49:28-33)
  VIII. Oracle Against Elam (49:34-39)

Oracle to Pharaoh's Army (46:2-12)

This oracle celebrates the defeat of the Egyptian armies at the battle of Carchemish in 605 B.C. when Egypt came north to aid Assyria against Babylon. Archaeological excavations at Carchemish (in modern Syria) have turned up many Egyptian objects from their occupation of the town shortly before the battle.

The battle iself was a turning point in the history of the ancient Near East. Assyria was demolished. Egypt was reduced to a secondary power, and Babylon was established as the dominant world power. Babylon held this position until the rise of the Persian empire in 539 B.C.

This oracle compares Egypt to the rising Nile (verses 7-8). Each year, the mighty Nile floods its banks, bringing fertility to the soil and life to Egypt. The Pharaoh hopes to *flood* the lands to the north with Egyptian might. Instead, Egypt is mortally wounded and shamed. *Ethiopia* (NRSV; NIV = *Cush*) is south of Egypt in modern Sudan. *Put* is probably part of modern Libya. *Lud* is perhaps Lydia in Asia Minor. Mercenaries from these countries fight in the Egyptian army (they are *hired soldiers*, according to Jeremiah 46:21).

Nebuchadrezzar in Egypt (46:13-26)

This oracle may refer to the battle of Carchemish (605 B.C.), to the battle of 601 B.C. between Egypt and Babylon, or to Nebuchadrezzar's invasion of Egypt in 568–567 B.C. (see Jeremiah 43:8-13). At none of these times, however, was Egypt completely conquered or left in ruins.

Verse 15 may refer to the bull-god of Memphis, in southern Egypt. An image of this bull may have been carried into battle by the Egyptians. The retreat or capture of such images in battle symbolizes the defeat of the people who worship the image.

Pharaoh's own troops refer to him condescendingly (verse 17) because of his defeat.

God proclaims an oath that all this shall come to pass (verse 18), using mountains in Israel as testimony to the truth of the oath. *Tabor* is a mountain above the plain of Jezreel in Northern Israel. *Carmel* is a mountain at the western end of the plain of Jezreel.

Gadfly (verse 20) may mean *butcher*.

Amon of Thebes is Amon-Ra, the imperial god of Egypt. Worship of this god takes place at the temple of Karnak in Thebes.

Consolation for Israel (46:27-28)

These verses are the same as Jeremiah 30:10-11. Here in chapter 46, this oracle contrasts the restoration of Israel with the destruction of Egypt. Verse 28 promises complete destruction to all the nations to which the

Israelites are exiled. Elsewhere, some nations (including Egypt) are promised eventual restoration (see 46:26; 48:47; 49:6, 39).

Oracle Against the Philistines (47:1-7)

Verse 1 introduces the oracle. *Before Pharaoh attacked Gaza* may refer to Egypt overrunning Kadytis (usually identified with Gaza) after the battle of Megiddo in 609 B.C. This oracle may also relate to Nebuchadrezzar's (*waters in the north,* verse 2) destruction of Ashkelon (verses 5, 7) in 604 B.C. Ashkelon is a city in the Philistine plain.

The Philistines are one of the Sea Peoples who came from Crete (*Caphtor,* verse 4) to settle on the coast of southern Palestine.

Tyre and Sidon are Phoenician cities allied with the Philistines.

Baldness and gashing (verse 5) refer to mourning rituals.

The Philistines and the Israelites had longstanding conflicts.

Oracles Against Moab (48:1-47)

This series of oracles is longer than any other in chapters 46–49. The individual oracles come from different periods of time. Moab and Israel had frequent conflicts from the time of the Exodus and Conquest of Canaan to the fall of Jerusalem.

In 602–601 B.C. when Jehoiakim rebelled against Babylon, Nebuchadrezzar sent Chaldeans, Syrians, Moabites, and Ammonites on raids against Judah (see Jeremiah 12:7-13; 2 Kings 24:2). Jeremiah 27:1-11 lists Moab among those plotting rebellion against Babylon. Moab may have joined in later uprisings during Zedekiah's reign which led to Nebuchadrezzar's invasion of Judah and the destruction of Jerusalem in 587 B.C. All these events may have prompted the messages of punishment against Moab.

Many place names associated with Moab are mentioned in these oracles.

Woe (verse 1 NIV; NRSV = *Alas*) is the traditional call to mourning. These oracles raise a funeral dirge over Moab (see verse 37, also *wail and cry*, verse 20, and *mourn,* verse 17).

Chemosh (verse 7) is the chief god of Moab.

The *curse* of verse 10 urges Moab's foe to carry out God's ordained punishment.

Dregs (verse 11) refers to the sediment that collects in the bottom of undisturbed containers of wine. Moab is compared to fine wine which has been left undisturbed but which will be poured out in destruction (verse 12).

Bethel (verse 13) is perhaps the former center of idol worship in southern Judah (see 1 Kings 12:28-29).

The *horn* and *arm* (verse 25) are symbols of strength.

Verses 29-46 contain passages also found in Isaiah 15-16 and Numbers 21 and 24 (for example, verse 29 in Isaiah 16:6; verses 31-33 in Isaiah 16:7-10; verses 45-46 in Numbers 21:28-29).

These oracles declare that Moab will suffer a reversal of circumstances. Once proud and fruitful, Moab has been devoured and destroyed by the enemy. The traditional merrymaking and singing that goes with the wine-making season will turn to shouts of fear (verse 33).

Moab was overrun by Arab tribes in approximately 650 B.C. It continued to exist as a state for another generation or two (see Jeremiah 27:3), and some refugees from Jerusalem fled there in 587 B.C. After this time, Moab was largely populated by nomads until settled life took hold again in the first century B.C.

Oracle Against the Ammonites (49:1-6)

This oracle may come from 602–601 B.C. at the time of Ammonite raids on Judah (see Jeremiah 12:7-13; 2 Kings 24:2). It also could have come from 595–594 B.C. during the possible rebellious plots of Zedekiah (see Jeremiah

27:3). *Ammon* is the brother of Moab and must be punished for its idolatry and violence.

Milcom (verse 1 NRSV; NIV = *Molech*) is the Ammonite national god.

When the Assyrians conquered and deported some of the tribes in northern Israel in 732 B.C., Ammonites moved into Israelite territory in Gad (Gilead).

Rabbah (verse 3) is the capital of Ammon.

Oracle Against Edom (49:7-22)

This oracle is closely related to oracles from the book of Obadiah, which was written sometime after 587 B.C. Verses 14-16 parallel Obadiah 1-4 and verses 9-10 parallel Obadiah 5-6.

Esau (verse 8) is considered the ancestor of the Edomites, who are brothers to Israel (see Deuteronomy 23:7-8). Israel and Edom shared friendly relations until the fall of Jerusalem in 587 B.C. Under pressure from Arab nomadic tribes entering their territory, the Edomites took advantage of Judah's weakened condition to move into southern Judah.

Teman (verse 7) and *Bozrah* (verse 13) are Edomite cities. Verse 12 refers to the cup of the wrath of God (see Jeremiah 25:28) which Israel and other nations must drink.

As in the case of Israel, the Edomites' false pride (verse 16) will be brought low. Verses 19-21 are also found in a slightly different form in Jeremiah 50:44-46 in an oracle against Babylon.

Oracle Against Damascus (49:23-27)

Damascus is the capital of the Aramean (or Syrian) kingdom (see Jeremiah 35:11; 2 Kings 24:1-4). It is a famous trading center located in an oasis in southern Syria. Damascus was conquered by Assyria in 732 B.C. and later became part of the Babylonian empire. The occasion for this oracle may have been the Syrians' participation in raids against Judah in 601 B.C.

The oracle portrays the proud and prosperous city as feeble, panic-stricken, and defeated. This is a witness to the prophetic conviction that human pride and strength always give way to God's strength.

Oracle Against Kedar and Hazor (49:28-33)

Nebuchadrezzar led a campaign against Arab tribes in the desert east of Judah in the winter of 599–598 B.C. *Kedar* and *Hazor* refer to desert-dwelling Arab tribes. They are not named in the list of Jeremiah 25:23-25, but other Arab groups and towns are named there among those who must drink the cup of God's wrath.

These nomads do not live in fortified cities (without *gates* or *bars*, verse 31). Nevertheless, the territory they roam in will not escape Nebuchadrezzar's destructive forces.

Oracle Against Elam (49:34-39)

Zedekiah became king of Judah in 597 B.C. In the winter of 596 B.C. Nebuchadrezzar attacked Elam, which is east of Babylonia. This oracle may come from the time of that military campaign.

The *bow of Elam* (verse 35) refers to the Elamites' fame as archers.

§ § § § § § §

The Message of Jeremiah 46-49

These oracles against the nations are related to a particular time in the history of Israel and of Israel's neighbors. However, they are more than just reactions to historical circumstances. These oracles have a larger perspective, as do all the oracles in Jeremiah. They describe Israel's and the other nations' relationship to God. What, then, do these oracles tell us about God's dealings with human beings? What do they tell us about what God is like?

§ God's nature and will are revealed through the words and actions of the prophet.

§ God acts in self-revelation to Israel and to other nations.

§ God is the Lord of all peoples.

§ God rules and judges the affairs and history of all humankind.

§ Israel has sinned and is punished for these sins.

§ Israel must choose to obey God and live or disobey and die.

§ God wants to be in relationship with all people.

§ God's will is for a loving and redeeming relationship with people. This relationship with Israel is realized in the new covenant.

§ § § § § § §

Jeremiah 50–52

Introduction to These Chapters

These last chapters in the book of Jeremiah contain oracles against Babylon (Jeremiah 50:1–51:64) and a historical narrative about Judah and Babylon from 588 B.C. to 560 B.C. (Jeremiah 52).

Here is an outline of chapters 50-52:
I. Oracles Against Babylon (40:1-51:64)
   A. God's judgment announced (50:1-46)
   B. Evil is coming to Babylon (51:1-58)
   C. Report of a sign act (51:59-64)
II. Israel Is Taken Into Exile (52:1-34)
   A. Jerusalem falls (52:1-11)
   B. The spoils of war (52:12-27)
   C. Israel in Exile (52:28-34)

Oracles Against Babylon (50:1-51:64)

This collection focuses on two main themes: the fall of Babylon and the return of the exiles to their homeland. The harsh judgment announced for Babylon (see for example, Jeremiah 50:14, 24) contrasts with Jeremiah's oracles concerning Nebuchadrezzar as God's servant (see Jeremiah 27:6) and with his view that Judah must submit to the yoke of Babylon (see Jeremiah 27:12). In support of these oracles of judgment, Jeremiah also proclaims that Babylon's rule will not last forever (see Jeremiah 27:7; 25:12-14).

The oracles concerning Babylon in the book of

Jeremiah treat Babylon as a necessary and timely instrument of punishment in God's hands (see Jeremiah 51:20-23). God uses Nebuchadrezzar and his armies to discipline Israel and her neighbors. However, Nebuchadrezzar is not above judgment himself. The oracles in Jeremiah reveal that the kings of Babylon, like the kings of Judah, are subject to God's plan for human history. Their military might may be useful to God for a time, but they, too, will eventually be defeated (see Jeremiah 50:44-46).

The oracles in Chapters 50-51 are not arranged chronologically or by theme. Some oracles are repeated. Announcements of disaster for Babylon are interrupted by announcements of restoration for Israel.

God's Judgment Announced (50:1-46)

At the time of the Exile, Babylon was a huge city, one of the wonders of the ancient world. It covered 500 acres and had a population of over 100,000.

Two walls, which were wide enough for chariots to be driven over the top of them, protected the city. The outer wall was ten miles long. A series of flooded ditches and artificial lakes around the walls gave further protection.

Many buildings in Babylon come from the time of Nebuchadrezzar. Inscriptions from his reign bearing the phrase *this great Babylon* have been found in archaeological excavations there. Nebuchadrezzar's palace contained the famous Hanging Gardens, which were one of the seven wonders of the ancient world.

Vast systems of canals brought water from the Euphrates River, which ran through the city, into the surrounding countryside for irrigation and transportation.

A reproduction of the Ishtar Gate, built by Nebuchadrezzar in 580 B.C., and of the great processional way may be seen today in a museum in East Berlin. These reproductions show the magnificence of Babylonian architecture. The front of the gate is decorated with pictures of bulls and dragons made from colored enameled bricks.

Jeremiah 50:35-38 lists other characteristics for which Babylon was famous. Babylon was mighty in war and in wealth. The water from her rivers and canals helped feed many people. The skill of her wise men and diviners became synonymous with the practice of magical arts.

The term *Chaldeans* is used throughout the oracles of Jeremiah 50-51 to mean *Babylonians* (see for example 50:1, 8, 35; 51:1, 24). Chaldea and Chaldeans at one time referred to an ethnic group living in tribes in an area of southern Babylonia. Nebuchadrezzar's father was a Chaldean. During Nebuchadrezzar's reign, the term *Chaldean* began to replace the term *Babylonian*. Later, *Chaldeans* was used to refer to people from Babylonia who practiced the arts of magic, astrology, and divination.

The oracles of judgment against Babylon in chapter 50 are found in verses 1-3, 8-16, 21-27, 28-30, 31-32, 35-40, and 41-46. These proclamations of punishment with their images of war and desolation are similar to proclamations against Israel elsewhere in the book of Jeremiah. (See, for example, Jeremiah 18:16; 19:8; 25:9, 11.)

The following terms are also found in these oracles:

—*Bel*, verse 2: Bel is the title of Marcuk (Merodach), Babylon's state god. The title indicates the supremacy of the god in a certain place and the god's sphere of influence.

—*Merodach*, verse 2: Merodach is the Hebrew name for Marduk. In Babylonian religion, Marduk is king and is honored as the creator of nature and humans.

—*Merathaim*, verse 21: In this form, the word means *double rebellion*. It is a play on the name of a region in southern Babylonia to show that Babylon is a *twofold rebel*.

—*Pekod*, verse 21: Pekod means *punishment*. Here it is used as a play on the name of an eastern Babylonian tribe.

The oracles concerning Israel's restoration are in verses 4-5, 6-7, 17-20, and 33-34. Israel will repent, will return to the homeland and sin no more, and will find rest. Rest for Israel has to do with the fulfillment of God's promises of blessing.

Evil Is Coming to Babylon (51:1-58)

In the oracles of Chapter 51, the judgment against Babylon is spoken of as being in the future (for example, verses 1-2) and as accomplished (for example, verses 8, 12-13). Two voices are heard in these oracles—the voice of the Lord and the voice of those witnessing Babylon's destruction.

In verses 1-4, 20-23, 24-33, 36-37, 38-44, 45-49, 52-53, and 57-58 God speaks to Babylon and speaks about Babylon. Though Nebuchadrezzar and his armies are God's *war club* of judgment (verses 20-23), they have done *evil* (verses 24, 49) and are idol worshipers (verse 52).

In verses 5-10, 11-14, 15-19, 34-35, 50-51, and 54-56 those people who have been *swallowed* by Babylon (verse 34) are heard. They offer a hymn of praise (verses 15-19, also in Jeremiah 10:12-16) to the greatness of God, and they speak of Babylon's desolation. They also remind the exiles to remember God and Jerusalem even though they are far from home (verses 50-51).

Report of a Sign Act (51:59-64)

These verses report a sign act that Jeremiah commissions Seraiah to carry out for him in Babylon. A collection of oracles against Babylon was made in approximately 594–593 B.C. It was sent to Babylon as a sign of Babylon's future destruction. Some of these oracles may be included in chapters 50–51.

Ararat, Minni, and Ashkenaz (verse 27) are peoples living north of Babylonia who were conquered by the Medes early in the sixth century B.C.

The *Medes* (verses 11, 28) are a people living northeast of Babylonia who helped the Babylonians conquer Assyria. In 560 B.C., there was an expectation in the Near East that the Medes would attack Babylon, which was going through a time of civil strife. The Medes did not attack then, but they were a part of Cyrus the Persian's successful campaign against Babylon in 539 B.C.

The oracles of chapters 50–51 declare that Babylon will be set afire and her walls leveled (verse 58). It is said that her ruins will be fit only for wild beasts (verse 37:50-39). All these things happened to Jerusalem, but not to Babylon.

Babylon was taken in 539 B.C. by the forces of Cyrus, King of Persia, but the city of Babylon was not destroyed. The city remained an important government and commercial center under the Persians and in the empire of Alexander the Great (356–323 B.C.). However, Alexander's successor built a new capital not far from Babylon. The new city gradually attracted all of Babylon's population. By the first century B.C., only a small group of astronomers and magicians still lived in the ancient city. So Babylon died by neglect and disinterest rather than by the sword. The city was left in ruins, but not in the way the oracles proclaimed.

Israel Is Taken into Exile (52:1-34)

The history in chapter 52 is much like the historical narrative in 2 Kings 24:18–25:30. It complements the reports in Jeremiah 39:1-10 and 40:7–43:7 concerning Judah's defeat.

This appendix shows that Jeremiah's prophecies concerning Jerusalem and Zedekiah came true. It ends on a hopeful note by telling of the favor Jehoiachin eventually was shown in Babylon in 560 B.C. (verses 31-34). The addition of this chapter to the book of Jeremiah also shows that the final collection of the prophet's words happened after 560 B.C.

Jerusalem Falls (52:1-11)

Zedekiah and the people of Israel angered God to the point that they were *cast out from his presence*. They were cast out of Zion and the Temple, thh symbol of God's presence with them. However, they were not completely or forever out of God's presence. Jeremiah has proclaimed that the people may find God in their hearts, because God's will is to establish a new relationship with them (see Jeremiah 29:10-14).

The Spoils of War (52:12-27)

The siege of Jerusalem lasted from January 588 B.C. to July/August 587 B.C. In August 587 B.C., Jerusalem was burned, the Temple stripped of its treasures, Temple officials and military leaders executed, and all but the poorest people taken captive.

A *cubit* is approximately eighteen inches.

The *pomegranate* (verses 22-23) was a common fruit in Palestine. It was frequently pictured in decorations as a symbol of fruitfulness and fertility.

Israel in Exile (52:28-34)

The three deportations listed here are dated according to Nebuchadrezzar's years as king. They are 597 B.C. (verse 28) after Jehoiakim's revolt, 587 B.C. after Zedekiah's revolt (verse 29), and 582–581 B.C. after Gedaliah's assassination (verse 30). The total of 4,600 persons probably does not include women and children.

Nebuchadrezzar's successor brought Jehoiachin out of prison and allowed him to sit in the palace in the company of other vassal kings. However, he was not allowed to return to Judah.

§ § § § § § §

The Message of Jeremiah 50-52

The oracles concerning Babylon in the book of Jeremiah treat Babylon as a necessary and timely instrument in God's hands. What does Jeremiah teach us about King Nebuchadrezzar's relationship to God and about Babylon's role in God's plan for history?

§ Nebuchadrezzar is God's servant and holds power over other nations at God's discretion.

§ God uses Nebuchadrezzar and his armies to discipline Israel and her neighbors.

§ Nebuchadrezzar is not above judgment himself.

§ The kings of Babylon, like the kings of Judah, are subject to God's plan for human history and to God's judgment.

§ The military power of Babylon's kings may be useful to God for a time, but they too will eventually be defeated.

If Babylon may only look toward future defeat, toward what may Israel look?

§ Israel's sins will be pardoned and the people will sin no more.

§ The people will return to their land and live in plenty.

§ Israel will be at "rest": war will be over, the land and people will be fruitful, the people will have a new peace of mind and contentment coming from a close relationship with God.

§ § § § § § §

Jeremiah—Conclusion

Jeremiah was a prophet, *one who has been called* by God. He was called to speak to the people of Israel in the context of a particular historical situation. During the years of Jeremiah's prophecy, Israel faced the end of life as an independent nation. Jeremiah brought the people a word that interpeted what was happening to them in light of God's demands and promises. The focal point of these demands and promises was the covenant.

Jeremiah spoke to the people about their relationship to God established in the covenant at Sinai. The covenant was more than just part of Israel's history. Their identity as a people was bound up in the covenant relationship with God. By this relationship and the memory of the Sinai experience, Israel was to find her way.

Jeremiah called on Israel to remember the past as the basis for interpreting the present and anticipating the future. The explanation for the tragedy of the people of Israel lay in God's sovereign power, justice, and faithfulness. The covenant agreement was both the basis for their punishment and the ground of their hope.

A new community would be established, based on a new covenant, a new saving act by God on Israel's behalf. Israel had shown her inability to abide by the old covenant, but the relationship to God established in the old covenant was not completely broken. On the basis of God's past loving kindness and justice this new covenant will be established.

The new covenant of faith will be an inward and personal relationship to God. The people will have a new heart engraved with God's statutes. Through the people's intimate knowledge of God, the new community will be born.

Jeremiah struggled and suffered with his people through the long years of his prophetic ministry. The punishment he proclaimed came to pass. The new covenant he announced took root and flowered in the coming of Jesus Christ.

Introduction to Lamentations

The book of Lamentations is a series of five poems that mourn the ruin of Jerusalem and the suffering of her people. These poems were written in response to the destruction of the city by the Babylonians in 587 B.C. Hundreds of people, including the king and his court, were either killed or were forceably deported to Babylon. Details of the siege and its aftermath are found in the books of Jeremiah and 2 Kings. The book of Lamentations records the emotional, psychological, and religious impact of this loss on the people of Israel.

The five poems voice the people's grief and sorrow and express their horror at what happened to them and to their homeland. The poems also acknowledge God as the power behind Israel's downfall. They ask, *What is the meaning of this tragedy?*

The Author of Lamentations

The poems of Lamentations are the work of a single author. Both Jewish and Christian tradition at one time named Jeremiah as this author. This view was, in part, based on 2 Chronicles 35:25. However, the general view today is that Chronicles refers to laments Jeremiah wrote that are not in the book of Lamentations. We do not know the name of the person who wrote Lamentations.

The events described in Lamentations are seen from the perspective of someone living in Judah from 587 B.C. to 538 B.C. when the exiles were given permission to return to Judah. These were harsh years for Judah, a time of economic hardship and spiritual reassessment. The people struggled to feed themselves and to come to terms with what had happened to them. The poems of Lamentations were composed over a period of years during this time.

All the poems were probably written or adapted for use in public worship services on days of fasting and mourning. In particular, these poems would have been used at the annual service held in remembrance of Jerusalem's destruction. An editor (who may or may not be the author) collected the poems and put them in order. Perhaps these laments were once part of a larger collection of worship materials.

The Form of the Poems

The five poems in Lamentations are laments, as the title suggests. Such poems are frequently found elsewhere in the Old Testament, since one-third of the Old Testament is poetry. Psalms, Proverbs, Song of Solomon, Lamentations, Obadiah, Micah, Nahum, Habakkuk, and Zephaniah are almost entirely poetry. The greater parts of Job, Isaiah, Hosea, Joel, and Amos are poetry, and Jeremiah is about one-half poetry.

Four of the five laments (chapters 1-4) are acrostic poems. In an acrostic poem, each of the twenty-two letters of the Hebrew alphabet appears in order at the beginning of each line or stanza. In English, we would compose an acrostic poem with the first line beginning with A, the second with B, the third with C, and so on. Such a form helps someone in memorizing a poem. This form also helps its writer express the completeness of grief and despair or of hope and faith. It lets the poet express "everything from A to Z," so to speak. Lamentations 5 is not an acrostic poem, but it does have twenty-two lines.

Laments express the sorrow or despair of individuals (for example, Jeremiah 11:18–12:6) and of whole communities (for example, Lamentations 5). Sometimes a community is personified as an individual (for example, Lamentations 1:18-19). Having one voice speak for the community expresses the tragedy on a personal level for each member of that community.

Laments are written in response to a disaster or the threat of a diaster. They usually have these parts:

1. the situation of the lamenter is described
2. sin is confessed
3. God is called on to act on behalf of the lamenter
4. faith in God is affirmed
5. God is praised.

Funeral laments, often accompanied by music, are composed for the dead (see for example, 2 Samuel 1:18-27). The dead are eulogized, their passing is mourned, or, in the case of an enemy, a death is celebrated. Funeral laments also offer consolation to those who are grieving. The poems of lamentations mourn for the people of Israel individually and as a community.

Lamentations in the Church

By the end of the second century B.C., Lamentations was included in the part of the Hebrew Scripture known as the *Writings*. After its inclusion in the Hebrew Bible, it became part of the Christian Old Testament.

Because the poems of Lamentations are regarded as sacred Scripture by both Christians and Jews, the poems became more than a defeated community's remembrance and reflection. The poems provide expressions of sorrow that have been and will be used by other mourners. Lamentations also gives us plenty of "food for thought" on how faith in God relates to what happens to God's people in this world.

In Jewiswh tradition and practice, Lamentations is read during the public mourning in the Hebrew month of Ab (July/August). This mourning commemorates the fall of Jerusalem in 587 B.C. Lamentations is also read by Jews every Friday afternoon at the Wailing Wall in the old city of Jerusalem.

In Christian congregations, Lamentations is traditionally read during Holy Week to reflect on the sufferings of Jesus before his crucifixion.

Lamentations 1–5

Introduction to These Chapters

The book of Lamentations shows how the worshiping community of Judah tries to deal with its suffering after the catastrophe of 587 B.C. In later years, Jewish rabbinical philosophers concluded that suffering serves divine purposes: it purifies, it teaches, and it is an agency of God's plan. The poems of Lamentations reflect a similar view of suffering. The people of Judah, though once rebellious, are now ready to confront their tragedy and find their way back to God.

Here is an outline of the book of Lamentations:
  I. Jerusalem Laments Her Miserable State (1:1-22)
 II. Lament over the Anger of the Lord (2:1-22)
III. Personal Lament and Prayer (3:1-66)
 IV. Lamentation over the Siege of Jerusalem (4:1-22)
  V. A Communal Plea for Mercy (5:1-22)

Jerusalem Laments Her Miserable State (1:1-22)

Two voices are heard in this lament—that of the poet (third-person) describing what has happened, and that of Jerusalem personified as a woman (first-person). To the Jews, Jerusalem is not just buildings or a place. The city is as a living being and a beloved member of the family of the people of Israel. Thus, the city speaks for all her inhabitants. They are as one in their misery.

The poet tells of Jerusalem's fate in verses 1-11a and

verse 17. The city speaks of its misery in verses 11b-16 and verses 18-19. In verses 20-22, the widow-Jerusalem offers a prayer asking God to take notice of her distress. The meter of the poem is that typically used in the Hebrew lament. Its three-beat plus two-beat rhythm is evident even in the English translation:

How sits so lonely the city—once populous;
A widow has she become—the queen of peoples;
The princess among princes—is a slave.

(Lamentations 1:1)

The word *how* (also translated *alas*) is often used to begin a poem that describes a striking change from happiness to grief or from greatness to misery. (For example, see Lamentations 1:1; 2:1; 4:1; Jeremiah 9:19; 48:17.) This exclamation expresses the speaker's astonishment and grief at such a change.

The day of the Lord (verses 12, 21) has brought a striking reversal of circumstances for Judah. Jerusalem was once a mighty city full of people, a place for worship and feasting. Now the city is empty and ruined. The people who were not killed by the enemy or carried into exile are starving to death.

Unclean foreigners have violated the Temple (verse 10; see also Deuteronomy 23:1-3; Ezekiel 44:9). Jerusalem's precious things (verses 7, 10), her Temple treasures, are gone.

Jerusalem is portrayed as both a widow (verse 1) and as a harlot (verses 8-9). Widows and orphans were among the most defenseless and pitied people in Israel. Harlots were among the most despised.

People trade their personal possessions (*treasures,* verse 11) for food.

This poem is the result of deep soul-searching and reflection. In the midst of such abject sorrow and misery, the poet has been able to reflect on the meaning of these circumstances. The chaos and torment of life in Jerusalem is described in the discipline of poetry. Within this disciplined expression, the poet declares the cause of the chaos and torment: *The Lord is in the right, for I have rebelled against his word* (verse 18, also verses 5, 8, 9, 14, 20, 22 NRSV). Through the poet, the people acknowledge their transgressions. They make the connection between their sin and what has happened to them. The people of Israel can now see Jeremiah's messages about sin and punishmenmt from the perspective of defeat and despair. However, the people are not abandoned. They still may call on the Lord out of their miserable state and seek comfort in God's presence. The refrain *there is no one to comfort me* appears five times in this poem (verses 2, 9, 16, 17, 21 NIV). Comfort is consolation and relief from distress. The people are in mourning and there are no sympathetic friends to offer support and comfort. (See Jeremiah 16:5-8 concerning help given in time of grief.) Israel may now turn only to God.

Lament over the Anger of the Lord (2:1-22)

Israel's guilt before God is confessed in the lament in chapter 1. The effects of God's righteous wrath against Israel because of this guilt are described in chapter 2.

Verses 1-17 describe what has happened to the city and the people because of God's anger.

Verses 18-19 call on the people to cry to God for mercy because of the destruction.

Verses 20-22 are a prayer calling on God to see the devastation of the people.

The *splendor of Israel* (verse 1) may be Jerusalem (see Isaiah 13:19) which is cast down like a falling star (see for example, Isaiah 14:12).

God's *footstool* (verse 1) is the Temple (see also Ezekiel 43:7; Isaiah 60:13; Psalm 132:7).

God's *right hand* (verse 3) is a symbol of strength and protection.

Verse 4 means those desirable to the eye of those who are good looking.

Verse 6 is about the Temple. God has destroyed the Temple as people destroy booths set up temporarily in in harvest fields.

The imagery of verse 8 comes from the actions of a builder who marks off lines for construction. In contrast, God marks off lines for planned destruction.

The *law* (verse 9 NIV; NRSV = *guidance*) refers to priestly instruction. This verse declares that God no longer comes to the people through political leaders, priests, or prophets.

The people are in mourning (verses 10-11) and are starving (verse 12).

(On hissing, wagging the head, clapping, and gnashing of teeth, verses 15-16, see the explanation of Jeremiah 18:13-17.)

In verses 20-22 the people cry to God to see the horrible results of the day of God's anger.

Verse 14 shows the results of serious theological reflection. The poet confesses that Israel listened to false prophets and confirms what Jeremiah said about these false prophets (see Jeremiah 23:9-15; 29:8-9). This confession, in effect, admits the people of Israel put their confidence in false promises. The false prophets assured the people that God would never destroy the Temple and would never allow David's royal dynasty to end.

The poet recognizes that the hope for Israel's future lies in confession of sin. Iniquity must be exposed and confessed. Punishment must be accepted as the result of God's righteous judgment. In this way, Israel's faith is not demolished but strengthened. The people can find their way back to God, and in God they can find their well-being.

Personal Lament and Prayer (3:1-66)

This poem is a triple acrostic in which each letter of the Hebrew alphabet is used three times before going on to the next letter.

In this lament, the poet describes his distress (verses

JEREMIAH AND LAMENTATIONS

1-20) and the hope he has in God (verses 21-24). He confesses God's justice and righteousness (verses 25-39) and the sins of the people, and pleads with God for punishment of his enemies (verses 40-66). The descriptions of suffering in verses 1-16 are similar to descriptions found in psalms of lament (for example, Psalm 89:32, *rod*; Psalm 107:10-11, *darkness*) and in Job (Job 10:21-22, *darkness*; see also Amos 5:18 on the darkness of God).

The poet speaks as an individual sufferer. He describes his affliction and then moves on to resignation, repentance, and prayer. This journey of the poet is complex and not without its human ambiguities. He asks why anyone should complain about punishment for sins (verse 39), and then confesses his sins (verse 42). But then he asks God's vengeance on those who executed the punishment because a wrong has been done to him (verse 59). The poet does indeed complain and does not want his enemies to receive better treatment from God than he does. When someone is in the depths of the pit, it is easier to ask for compassion for oneself than for one's enemies.

Despite this note of vengeance, the poet points the way out of the depths for the people of Israel because his confession and prayer are their confession and prayer. The poet says that because both good and bad come from God (verses 37-38, 43-45) the people may turn to God in repentance and expect God to hear their plea.

Lament over the Siege of Jerusalem (4:1-22)

This lament contrasts Jerusalem's former splendor with the condition of the city after the Babylonian siege. The poet speaks as a witness to the devastation of the city, describing the fate of the common people and the leaders (verses 1-20). The lament ends with a curse on Edom and a blessing on Zion (verses 21-22).

Blame for the people's miserable fate is especially laid

on the prophets and priests (verses 13-16), though the sin of the people is also confessed (verse 22).

The *gold* of verse 1 is figurative. It represents the people of Zion (verse 2), who are worth more than gold but are treated as worthless broken pottery.

The effects of famine are described in verses 3-10. The mothers of Jerusalem do not or cannot feed their children and are like the proverbially neglectful ostrich toward their young (verse 3).

Purple clothes (verse 5) are worn by the rich and by royalty.

In contrast to Sodom's quick destruction (verse 6), Jerusalem's agony is long and drawn out.

Her *princes* or *youths* (verse 7) once had clear fair skin and their bodies were a healthy reddish color. Their *appearance* (NIV; NRSV = *hair*) is perhaps their beard which is compared to a dark blue gemstone. In verse 8, the contrast to this healthy picture is striking.

Cannibalism (verse 10) is listed in Deuteronomy 28:53-57 as one of the curses that will come upon Israel for disobedience to the covenant.

The priests and prophets are responsible for the shedding of innocent blood (see also 2:14; 2 Kings 21:16; Jeremiah 22:17; Ezekiel 22:6, 27), and are made unclean by this blood. They (and the people) are unclean and are treated as untouchable lepers. God's face, God's benevolent presence, is turned away from Israel.

Verses 17-18 describe the last days of the siege when food in the city was gone and no help was in sight.

Verses 19-20 describe Zedekiah's flight from Jerusalem and his capture by the Babylonians. (See also Jeremiah 52:6-9; 2 Kings 25:3-6).

The book of Obadiah provides the background for the curse on Edom in verses 21-22 (see Obadiah verse 1; also Jeremiah 49:7-22). Here, as in Lamentations 1:21-22 and 3:60-66, the poet prays for divine justice to overtake his enemies just as it has overtaken Israel. Israel's punishment is accomplished, however, and she can hope and pray for better days, but there is no hope for Edom. Edom will drink the cup of God's wrath and her sins will be uncovered just as drunken soldiers expose themselves.

A Communal Plea for Mercy (5:1-22)

Chapter 5 is a prayer of the community that describes the people's hardship under Babylonian rule, confesses the people's sin, and calls on God for mercy. This prayer is similar to communal laments found in the Psalms. (See for example, Psalms 44; 60; 74; 80.)

Many stanzas in this poem use synonymous parallelism in which one line repeats, or parallels, the thought of the first. Verse 2 is an example of this kind of parallelism: *Our inheritance has been turned over to strangers, / our homes to aliens.*

Verse 7 is an example of synthetic parallelism, in which the second line supplements or completes the first: *Our fathers sinned . . . ; / and we bear their punishment.* Both these types of parallelism between lines are commonly used in Hebrew poetry.

The people's sense of *disgrace* (verse 1) over what has happened to them is as strong as their physical distress. The people of Israel have a strong sense of honor and of the proper order of life. They complain of shame and disgrace when their honor is degraded and this proper order is upset.

No rest (verse 5) means *we are weary.* No rest also means that one benefit of Israel's status as God's people has been taken away. The established order has been upset. Israel believes that rest, particularly from enemies, is part of God's blessings to the people of Israel in the Promised Land. (See also Deuteronomy 12:10; 25:19; 2 Samuel 7:1, 11.)

Israel's past political and economic alliances with Egypt and Assyria (verses 6-7) are condemned. They are blamed, in part, for Israel's present condition of being under Babylonian domination.

Slaves (verse 8) are Babylonian officials who supervise the province of Judah for Nebuchadrezzar.

Verses 9-12 describe the lawlessness and famine in Jerusalem and Judah after the siege. Verse 12 may also mean *Their* [the Babylonians'] *hands hanged our princes.*

The *crown* (verse 16) is a symbol of nationhood (see also Jeremiah 13:18).

In verse 16 the people confess *we have sinned!* It is not just their fathers who went astray (verse 7). They, too, have sinned against the covenant. Jeremiah 3:25 says the same thing: *We have sinned against the Lord our God, we and our fathers, from our youth even to this day.*

Because of sin, Mount Zion is in ruins. Zion is the symbol of God's presence with the people of Israel. It is God's *footstool* (see 2:1). However, God no longer dwells there. The Temple area is a haunt for wild animals. One of the curses traditionally associated with ancient treaties and covenants was that wild animals would make their home in the ruined city of the partner that broke the covenant.

Verse 19 is a little hymn of praise to God's eternal dominion and strength. This hymn leads into questions in verses 20 and 22. *Why?* and *How long?* are commonly asked in communal laments. (See also Psalms 74:1, 11; 79:5, 10; 80:12.)

In verse 21, the people turn to God, asking God to bring them back and help them repent (see also Jeremiah 31:18). They acknowledge God's sovereignty and admit their need for God's redemptive action in their lives.

In some Hebrew manuscripts of Lamentations, verse 21 is repeated after verse 22. Also, in synagogue readings, verse 21 is read after verse 22 so that the reading of this passage will end on a penitent and hopeful note rather than on one of questioning and doubt.

§ § § § § § §

The Message of Lamentations 1-5

The poems of Lamentations came from Israel's attempts to find meaning in her suffering at the hands of the Babylonians. What does Israel discover in this search?

§ The people of Israel have sinned and must confess their sin.

§ Their suffering is a punishment from God for sin.

§ Yet, they still have a relationship and a future with God.

§ Though the Temple is gone, the people may seek God in public and private prayer and in worship.

§ They may call on God for help because God's justice includes both punishment and mercy.

§ § § § § § §

Lamentations—Conclusion

The book of Lamentations is full of complaints, to be sure. However, its aims are not limited to a description of suffering. These poems are an expression of Israel's humbleness and repentance in the face of a terrible national tragedy. The people of Israel, as individuals and as a community, had suffered in ways most of us can scarcely imagine. The poems of Lamentations helped them cope with this suffering because they could voice their pain together through the poetry. As a Jewish proverb says, "The one who suffers alone suffers most."

Israel never forgot her suffering and loss. The future brought other such times to God's people, but Israel's faith was not destroyed. The people of Israel came to recognize that what Jeremiah said was true: God's ultimate redemptive purposes for God's people will be fulfilled.

Glossary of Terms

Abarim: A mountainous region at the western edge of the plateau of northern Moab, overlooking the Dead Sea and the Jordan Valley. Mount Nebo is the principal peak and from it Moses viewed the land of Canaan.

Abomination: Anything that is ritually or ethically offensive to God and to God's people.

Ai: No place of that name is known in Ammon. Instead of *Ai,* some translations read *the city is laid waste* or, *the destroyer has come up.*

Ammon: Territory in the Transjordan (land east of the Jordan River) roughly bounded by the River Jabbok on the north and the river Arnon on the south, occupied by a Semitic people known as Ammonites. Was Israelite territory under David.

Anathoth: Jeremiah's birthplace in the territory of Benjamin, probably the present-day village of Anata, two miles northeast of Jerusalem.

Arab: From a Hebrew word meaning *ambush*; it is also translated *bandit*; generally indicates nomadic tribes living in Arabia.

Arabia: From a word meaning *desert* or *steppe*, a large peninsula in southwest Asia. The northwest portion is often mentioned in Scripture. Its caravan routes carried Arabian goods as well as goods from Africa and India.

Ark of the Covenant: The container for the stone tablets of the Law; also thought of as a portable throne for the presence of God, and the embodiment of God's presence with the people of Israel.

Arpad: A city and minor state in northern Syria. The Bible always mentions it along with Hamath as an example of places destroyed by the Assyrians.

Asherim: Plural form of the name of the pagan goddess Asherah; it can also mean the idols by which she was represented.

Assayer and Tester: Someone who tests ores for their gold or silver content.

Assyria: A civilization which, along with Babylonia, flourished in Mesopotamia from approximately 2500–2000 B.C. to its defeat by Babylonia in approximately 612 B.C. Assyria took control of the Northern Kingdom (Israel) in 722 B.C.

Baal: A Canaanite fertility God.

Babylon: Replaced Assyria as the dominant Mesopotamian civilization in 612 B.C. until its absorption by Persia in 539 B.C.; took control of the Southern Kingdom (Judah) in 598 B.C.

Balm in Gilead: Resin from the styrax tree, produced especially in the north Transjordan region of Gilead, widely used for medicinal purposes.

Bashan: The region east and northeast of the Sea of Galilee and east of the Jordan River; it was well adapted to growing wheat and cattle and was famous for its groves of oak trees; was taken by the Israelites from the Amorites.

Bel: The title of Merodach/Marduk, the state god of Babylon, which means *he who possesses, subdues, rules;* the title indicates the god's power over a certain place.

Benjamin: Son of Jacob and brother of Joseph; also the territory given his tribe, which was taken into the Southern Kingdom of Judah under Josiah.

Bethhaccherem: Identified with modern Ramet Rahel, two miles south of Jerusalem.

Booth: A temporary shelter constructed of branches and vines, used in pastures and on battlefields; the Feast of Booths is one of Israel's great annual festivals, celebrating the end of the agricultural year and recalling Israel's wilderness pilgrimage.

Bozrah: Probably the strongest city in northern Edom, a

fortress that guarded an important road and the approaches to copper mines in the area.

Buz: A tribe and/or territory in northwest Arabia.

Carmel: Mount Carmel is a prominent peak on the coast of Palestine, known for its beauty and fertility.

Chaldeans: Chaldea and Chaldeans were a region and a tribal group in southern Babylon; during Nebuchadrezzar's reign, Chaldean came to mean the same as Babylonian.

Chemosh: Name or title of the Moabite god; Solomon built a temple to Chemosh (1 Kings 11:7) which Josiah abolished (2 Kings 23:13).

Covenant: A solemn promise between two partners which is sealed with an oath and/or a symbolic action. The basic terms of God's covenant with Israel are found in the Ten Commandments (see Exodus 20:1-17; Deuteronomy 5:1-21).

Cut Corners of Hair: Ancient heathen practices for mourning the dead included shaving the head, cutting hair at the temples, and cutting the beard; these practices were forbidden to Israelites (see Leviticus 19:27).

Cyprus: Also called Kittim; an island in the Mediterranean Sea approximately forty miles from Asia Minor and sixty miles from Syria; famous for its copper.

Damascus: A city in Syria northeast of the Sea of Galilee, in an oasis watered by rivers and canals; an important center of commerce and religion.

Dan: The northernmost city in Israel.

Dedan: Perhaps a settlement of Dedanites living in Edom; Dedanites were an important commercial and trading people who lived in northwest Arabia to the southeast of Edom.

Diviners: Those who practice divination, the art of identifying the will and intentions of the gods; the Babylonians were the first to develop this art to an almost scientific discipline.

Edom: The land and people to the south and east of Judah, named after a red rock and called the *red region.*

Egypt: A land in northwest Africa along the Nile River; one of the earliest and most powerful civilizations of the ancient Near East.

Ekron: An important Philistine city in northern Palestine.

Elam: A region east of the Euphrates-Tigris Rivers on the slopes of the Iranian plateau. Susa was its capital.

Ephraim, Mount: In the hill country of central Palestine, the territory given to the tribe of Ephraim, Joseph's son.

Esau: The son of Isaac and Rebekah, the elder twin brother of Jacob and the traditional ancestor of the Edomites; the *calamity of Esau* may refer to his trading away his birthright and to the loss of his father's blessing (see Genesis 25–27).

Ethiopia: The ancient name for the territory south of Egypt, the area of present-day Sudan; also called *Cush.*

Euphrates: The largest river in western Asia, along with the Tigris; a major river of Mesopotamia.

Gad: The seventh son of Jacob, also his tribe; settled land east of the Jordan and west of Ammon.

Gall: A bitter and poisonous herb, mentioned with wormwood in the context of bitterness and tragedy.

Gareb: A suburb or quarter of Jerusalem, possibly on the southwest hill.

Gaza: An important Philistine city in southwestern Palestine; the land gateway for commercial and military traffic between Egypt and Asia.

Gedaliah: Governor of Judah under Babylonian rule, 587–582 B.C.

Goah: A suburb of Jerusalem.

Gomorrah: A city destroyed by God along with Sodom for its wickedness, probably now located under the waters of the southern part of the Dead Sea.

Hamath: An important town in Syria on the Orontes River, taken by the Assyrians and Babylonians.

Hazor: May be a place or a group of tribes in the Arabian desert east of Palestine.

Hedges: Thorn hedges or fences constructed to protect vineyards.

Heshbon: An important city in northern Moab, fifty miles east of Jerusalem; occupied at times by Israelites, Ammonites, and Amorites.

Hezekiah: King of Judah (715–687 B.C.).

High Places: Canaanite sanctuaries, either open-air or roofed, which were on high hills.

House of Israel, of Jacob: Jacob, also called Israel, was the son of Isaac and Rebekah, *house of* . . . means his descendants, the people of Israel.

Jehoiachin: Also called Jeconiah and Coniah, king of Judah (598–597 B.C.), carried into exile by Nebuchadrezzar.

Jehoahaz: King of Judah (609 B.C.), carried into captivity to Egypt by Pharaoh Neco.

Jehoiakim: King of Judah (609–598 B.C.), son of Josiah and brother of Jehoahaz.

Jericho: One of the oldest cities in the world, at the southern end of the Jordan Valley in a key defense position.

Josiah: King of Judah (640–609 B.C.).

Kedar: An area east and southeast of Israel, part of present-day Jordan and Saudi Arabia.

Lamentations: Poems used in the ritual of mourning or in times of danger by individuals and the community.

Manasseh: King of Judah (687–642 B.C.).

Media: An ancient area in northwestern Iran, first settled in 1400–1000 B.C.

Memphis: A major city in northern Egypt, thirteen miles south of Cairo.

Merodach/Marduk: The god of Babylon.

Mesopotamia: The cradle of civilization, the land between the Tigris and Euphrates Rivers, now in modern Iraq.

Milcom/Molech: The Ammonite national god.

Moab: A country east of the Dead Sea and south of the Jordan River.

Nebuchadrezzar/Nebuchadnezzar: King of Babylon (605–562 B.C.).

Negeb: A dry region in southern Canaan which runs from the Sinai Peninsula to the Dead Sea; the name sometimes means simply *south*. In ancient times, it had more vegetation and more settlements than it does now.

North: In general, north refers to any invader coming into

Israel from the north; major travel routes through Palestine ran north and south between the Mediterranean on the west and the desert on the east.

Oracle: In general, a divinely inspired message; specifically, a prophetic speech form.

Pathros: The *Land of the South,* southern Egypt.

Queen of Heaven: The Babylonian-Assyrian goddess Ishtar, whose worship was possibly introduced into Judah by Manasseh. This cult was popular with women who were restricted to an inferior role in the worship services to God. Offerings included wine and star-shaped or crescent-shaped cakes with the image of the goddess on them.

Rabbah: The capital of Ammon, the present-day Amman in Jordan.

Riblah: An ancient Syrian town north of Damascus; the military highways of Egypt and Mesopotamia crossed here.

Sackcloth: A garment made of goat's hair or camel's hair that was often worn as a symbol of mourning.

Samaria: The capital of the Northern Kingdom, also a region in the hill country of Palestine; conquered by Assyria in 721 B.C.

Sea, Bronze: Also called *molten sea* (1 Kings 7:23), a large vessel made of cast bronze which may have stood before the altar in the Temple in Jerusalem, and perhaps held water in which the priests washed.

Sheba: A country in southwest Arabia; its people were famous traders.

Shephelah: A foothill district west of the Judean highlands and east of the coastal plain; one of the major geographical divisions of Judah.

Shiloh: Located eighteen miles north of Jerusalem; a major Israelite shrine was here until its destruction in 1050 B.C.

Sidon: An ancient Phoenician seaport between Tyre and Beiruit; an agricultural, fishing, and trading center famous for its purple dye which was made from the murex shell.

Sihon: King of the Amorites, a Canaanite tribe living at times in the mountains of Judah and in an area east of the Jordan around Heshbon and Bashan.

Sodom: A very wicked city, destroyed along with Gomorrah, now under the southern part of the Dead Sea.

Tahpanhes: A city on the eastern frontier of northern Egypt.

Tarshish: A far-off port that exported fine silver, tin, iron, and lead; perhaps Sardinia or Tartessus in Spain.

Tekoa: A city in the highlands of Judah twelve miles south of Jerusalem.

Tema: A son of Ishmael (see Genesis 25:15); also the name of a city in northwest Arabia in an oasis at the junction of two important caravan routes.

Teman: The home of the Temanites, a clan descended from Esau; the largest city in central Edom.

Topheth (Valley of the Son of Hinnom): A place in the valley of the Son of Hinnom which runs east and west just south of Jerusalem; associated with pagan worship.

Tyre: An important Phoenician seaport in southern Phoenicia; famous for its navigators and traders.

Uphaz: A place mentioned in the Old Testament as a source of gold; its exact location is unknown.

Uz: An undefined area east of Palestine in the Syrian Desert.

Waistcloth: A loincloth, either worn loose like a skirt or pulled between the legs and tucked into the waist.

Wormwood: A plant with a bitter taste, often mentioned with gall in the context of bitterness and sorrow.

Zedekiah: (1) King of Judah (597–587 B.C.); (2) An exile, son of Maaseiah, condemned by Jeremiah for false prophecy.

Zimri: May refer to an Arabian tribe in the incense trade.

Zion: Originally the fortified hill of pre-Israelite Jerusalem; later came to mean both Jerusalem as the religious capital of Israel and the people of Israel as a religious community.

Guide to Pronunciation

Abarim: Ah-bah-REEM
Abomination: Ah-bah-mih-NAY-shun
Ai: EYE
Ammon: AM-mun
Anathoth: AN-uh-thothe
Arabia: Ah-RAY-bee-ah
Arpad: ARE-pahd
Ashdod: ASH-dod
Asherim: Ash-uh-REEM
Ashkelon: ASH-keh-lon
Assyria: A-SEER-ee-ah
Baal: Bah-ALL
Babylon: BAB-eh-lon
Bashan: Bah-SHAHN
Bethhaccherem: BETH-hah-KIR-um
Bozrah: BOHZ-rah
Buz: BUHZ
Carmel: Car-MEL
Chaldeans: Kal-DEE-ans
Chemosh: KAY-mosh
Cyprus: SIGH-pruss
Damascus: Duh-MASS-kus
Dedan: DEE-dan
Edom: EE-dum
Egypt: EE-gypt
Ekron: EHK-run
Elam: EE-lum
Ephraim: EE-frah-eem

Esau: EE-saw
Ethiopia: Ee-thee-OH-piah
Euphrates: You-FRAY-tees
Gareb: GAHR-eb
Gaza: GAH-zah
Gedaliah: Geh-dah-LIGH-uh
Gilead: GIH-lee-ad
Goah: GO-ah
Gomorrah: Guh-MORE-uh
Hamath: Ha-MAHTH
Hazor: HAH-tsore
Heshbon: HESH-bon
Hezekiah: Heh-zeh-KIGH-uh
Hilkiah: Hil-KIGH-uh
Jehoahaz: Jeh-HOE-ah-haz
Jehoiachin: Jeh-HOY-ah-kin
Jehoiakim: Jeh-HOY-ah-kim
Jericho: JEH-rih-koh
Josiah: Joh-SIGH-ah
Kedar: KAY-dar
Manasseh: Mah-NAS-seh
Marduk: MAR-duke
Media: ME-dee-ah
Memphis: MEM-fis
Merodach: MER-oh-dahk
Mesopotamia: Mes-soh-poh-TAY-mee-uh
Milcom: MILL-kahm
Moab: MOH-ab
Molech: MOH-leck
Nebuchadrezzar: Neh-buh-kah-DREZ-zer
Negeb: NEH-geb
Oracle: OR-ah-cul
Pashhur: PASH-er
Pathros: PATH-ros
Philistines: FILL-iss-teens
Rabbah: Rah-BAH
Rechabites: REH-kah-bites

Riblah: RIB-lah
Samaria: Sah-MARE-ee-ah
Sheba: SHE-bah
Shephelah: Sheh-FAY-lah
Shiloh: SHIGH-low
Sidon: SIGH-dun
Sihon: SEE-hun
Sodom: SOD-um
Syria: SEAR-ee-ah
Tahpanhes: TAH-puh-neez
Tarshish: Tar-SHEESH
Tekoa: Teh-KOE-ah
Tema: TAY-mah
Teman: TAY-mahn
Topheth: TOH-feth
Tyre: TIRE
Uphaz: YOU-faz
Uz: UHZ
Zedekiah: Zeh-deh-KIGH-uh
Zimri: ZIM-ree
Zion: ZYE-un

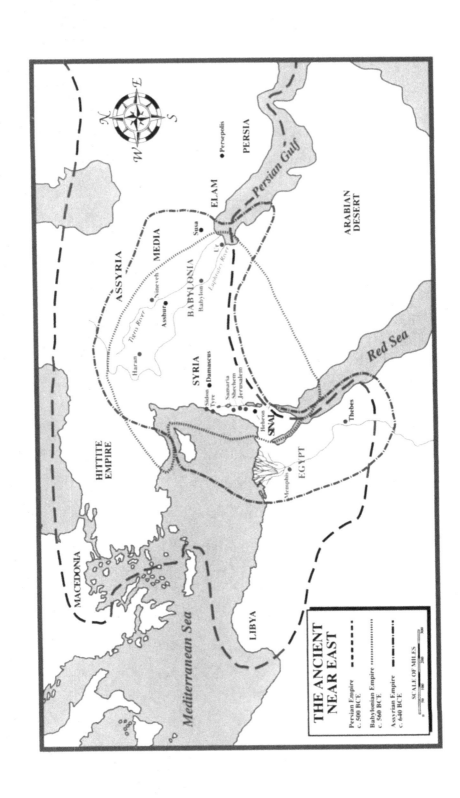

THE ANCIENT NEAR EAST

Persian Empire
c. 500 BCE

Babylonian Empire
c. 560 BCE

Assyrian Empire
c. 640 BCE

SCALE OF MILES

THE
KINGDOMS
OF ISRAEL
AND JUDAH

SCALE OF MILES

0   10   20   30   40

The
Great
Sea

ISRAEL

SAMARIA

River Jordan

Joppa

Bethel

JERUSALEM

Tokea

Moresheth

Gaza

PHILISTIA

Beersheba

JUDAH

Kadesh-
barnea

EDOM

KINGDOM OF
EGYPT

Elath

Sidon

Tyre

Dan

PHOENICIA

Damascus

KINGDOM OF
DAMASCUS

AMMON

Lake (Dead Sea)

MOAB

Arabian Desert

N
W   E
S

CPSIA information can be obtained at www.ICGtesting.com
Printed in the USA
LVOW01s2321190215

427593LV00009B/148/P

9 780687 026326